Starr Gate to the Tower

The Blackpool Tramway since 1960

Volume One

Rails

Starr Gate to the Tower

Brian Turner

The Blackpool Tramway since 1960

Volume One

Contents

First published 2014

Published by Rails Publishing
www.capitaltransport.com

Printed by Parksons Graphics

Foreword

With the opening of the Supertram system in April 2012, the Blackpool tramway entered a period of stability such as it had scarcely known since its 75th anniversary in 1960 - by chance the year that I started photographing the trams. So this seemed a good time to look at how the line had changed during that half century.

My plan was to make a photographic trip from Starr Gate to Fleetwood, but - as happens in Blackpool - this volume turned short when it reached the Tower. Those three miles have been divided into ten main sections, each of which is essentially chronological. The rest of the journey to Fleetwood will perhaps occupy another two volumes.

Although this is a book about the tramway rather than the tramcars, I've tried to select pictures that show the remarkable variety of cars which have been operated. For readers new to the subject, there's an all-time fleet list, whilst more details of the fleet can be found in my book *North Pier by Tram*.

The focus is on the tramway going about its everyday business, rather than on organised events such as processions and enthusiasts' tours, though a few of both do creep in from time to time.

Most of the pictures are my own, and as many as possible are in colour. But there are gaps in my coverage, particularly in the early years, when I was working mainly in black-and-white. I'm grateful, therefore, to Andrew Blood, David Christie, Peter Fitton, Malcolm King, Peter Langley, Ted Lightbown, Peter Makinson, Jean-Henri Manara, James Millington, Gary Mitchell, David Packer, Alan Robson, Clyde Shoebridge, Geoffrey Tribe, Paul Turner and Tony Wilson for additional photographs and information.

Here, then, is half a century of the Blackpool tramway as I saw it, with all its foibles, its unpredictability and - to me, at least - its endless fascination.

Brian Turner
Lytham
June 2014

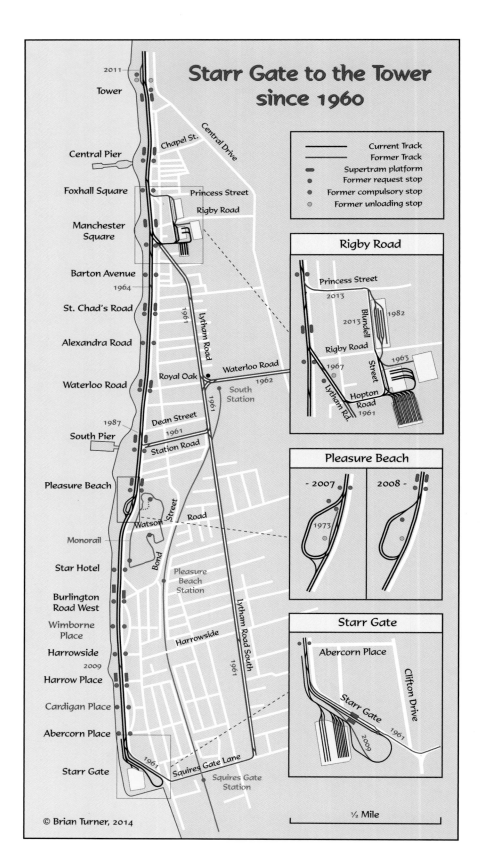

© Brian Turner, 2014

1. Starr Gate

Blackpool trams didn't reach Starr Gate until 1926, when an extension from Pleasure Beach was built along New South Promenade; the Lytham cars served the place from 1896 to 1937, though there was no-one much to serve in what were just empty sand-dunes. In 1938 the terminus was rebuilt as a turning circle, at the same time as a similar circle was built at Little Bispham on the Fleetwood Tramroad. Somehow the plans seem to have got mixed up, as Little Bispham was laid in Promenade style - with paved, unfenced, grooved rail - while Starr Gate resembled a lost fragment of the Fleetwood Tramroad marooned at the wrong end of the Promenade, complete with bullhead rail, concrete fencing and cattle guards.

Above Balloon car 724 stands at the unloading point - there wasn't an official stop sign - by the Tramroad-style gates and fence at Starr Gate on 29 July 1979 before pulling up to the shelter.

Street Track

The connecting line from New South Promenade along Starr Gate to join the Lytham St Annes tramway in Clifton Drive was laid in July 1928, but not connected to Squires Gate Lane until May 1932. The northbound track fell out of use in 1937, when the Lytham tramway closed. The other track remained until the Circular Tour ended in 1940, and was revived along with the Tour in 1957. The last Circular ran on 11 September 1960, but the track was used by enthusiasts' tours until it closed with the Squires Gate route on 29 October 1961.

Top Standard car 160 leaves the short single-track section on 22 May 1960. Coronation 324 (now preserved as 660) stands at the 1938 shelter.

Centre Twin-car 275 on 22 April 1961. (*Vic Nutton / Travelens*)

Below An evening Circular Tour car turns from Starr Gate onto Squires Gate Lane in 1960. The driver of a Standard Eight waits and watches - as well he might, since the scene would soon be part of history.

Above A long way from its Bispham home during an enthusiasts' tour on 4 June 1961, Pantograph car 170 edges round the curve from Starr Gate into Squires Gate Lane, between a Zephyr Zodiac and a pair of Co-op milk wagons exchanging loads, in a world innocent of yellow lines and parking wardens.

Below The end of the line. As the sun sets on 29 October 1961, Standard car 40 makes the last journey of all up Squires Gate Lane, raising valedictory sparks from the little-used overhead.

Standards at Starr Gate

Top Even in their heyday, Standard cars were never common at Starr Gate. In August 1961 car 49 is working a special to Cabin, which was as far as Standards normally ran, while Coronation 320 has just arrived from Fleetwood. No. 49 has been preserved at the National Tramway Museum since December 1962.

Centre No. 41 leaves the terminus on July 1960, passing the former air-raid shelter which served as public toilets. Three weeks later No. 41 split the points at Manchester Square while being towed back to depot, and never ran again.

Bottom Twilight for 147, which is just about to conclude its final run - an enthusiasts' tour on 29 October 1966 - before leaving for America, where it stayed until returning to Blackpool in 2000.

Railcoaches at Starr Gate

Top On a breezy 18 March 1961, a Brush railcoach – either 292 or 293 – stands at Starr Gate, which looks much as it did in 1938. The tram shelter and the building on the far right are both pre-war, the street lamps older still, being erected in 1926 to an 1893 design. The only evidence of modernity comes from the *Limited Stop* sign and orange bands added in 1960.

Centre A Bispham-bound railcoach pulls away from Starr Gate in January 1963, whilst 266 prepares to draw up to the tram stop. (*Colin McLeod*)

Below An unusual view of Starr Gate terminus on 4 November 1962, with railcoach 223 passing the old air-raid shelter and the AA caravan. The patrolman - with his motor-cycle combination parked next to the caravan - is having a quiet day with only a solitary Morris Minor to be seen. The tracks into Squires Gate lane are still there, minus wires. A new road junction was laid out at the beginning of 1964. (*Peter Fitton*)

Starr Gate Turning Circle

Top Although *Starr Gate* eventually prevailed as the destination, some cars showed *Clifton Drive* and others - like this Coronation - *South Promenade*. The bleak landscape makes this picture hard to date, though it must be around 1955, when the new cars started to lose their chrome-work and sliding windows, but still had swivel-head trolleys. (*Malcolm King collection*)

Centre During the bitterly cold January of 1963, Coronation 323 waits to leave for Fleetwood, ahead of Bispham Depot's Brush car 301 on the Starr Gate - Bispham service. (*Colin McLeod*)

Below The terminus lost a little of its emptiness in 1965 when Blackpool Council used 350 square yards of land inside the circle for a block of toilets to replace the air-raid shelter shown on page 8. The new block was served by a wide footpath, running right across the circle from the street to the car park, and crossing the tram tracks twice. Footpath and part of the tracks were lined with more Tramroad-style concrete fencing, and no less than twelve new sprung gates. Here Balloon 248 (later 711) passes the new fencing in 1967.

- 10 -

Starr Gate Turning Circle

Top The view from the car park on 24 July 1969, as Balloon 715 leaves the terminus. The overhead has been changed from span wires to bracket arms, probably when the toilet block was built in 1965. (*Clyde L. Shoebridge*)

Centre Further encroachment took place in 1970, when Arnold Palmer Enterprises leased a third of an acre inside the turning circle for a crazy-golf course. Balloon 707 stands between the golf course and the shelter on 29 July 1976. (*Geoffrey Tribe*)

Below A view of the golf course and the Tramroad-style gates on 12 April 1988. Engineering car 753, powered by its diesel engine, is attending to the overhead. Note the sand-shield on the disintegrating concrete fence.

- 11 -

Starr Gate Tram Shelter

Above After 42 years' service, the original steel shelter was in its final weeks when OMO car 5 loaded on 29 June 1980. One-man operation could be a slow process in summer, and the next car has already caught up with No. 5.

Centre Only a few panels of the 1938 shelter remain on 5 August 1980, with passengers boarding at a temporary stop. Balloon 723 shows *Thornton Gate via Cleveleys* in a non-standard style of blind.

Bottom A few weeks later, one of the usual (since 1972) Adshel shelters was erected, enlivened with a nice hand-painted notice. Jubilee 761 - working route (i.e. duty) 3 in one-man mode - waits on the morning of 12 December 1981. When this picture was taken, the thermometer at Squires Gate meteorological station showed six degrees Fahrenheit (-14.5 degrees Celsius), the coldest day ever recorded in Blackpool.

Top Another example of Tramroad style at Starr Gate - though short-lived and rarely photographed - was the station nameboard, seen here in fine condition on 13 June 1985, with the mayoral Daimler alongside curtained Standard car 40. (*Peter Fitton*)

Centre The box on the northbound track was an experiment to see whether grass-tracks on the continental style might be feasible on the Promenade; strictly it wasn't grass, but tiny ground-cover plants. Passing the box on 7 May 2009 is the Western Train, during its first test run since restoration (*see page 95*). Illuminations Tours ceased to run to Starr Gate some years ago, so the Train and its illuminated sisters are rare visitors these days. (*James Millington*)

Below In 1987 Fylde Borough Transport - successor to the Lytham St Annes tramways - introduced a *Beachcomber* minibus service between Starr Gate and the Gynn, in competition with the trams. On 28 May 1988, Blackpool Transport countered with their own *Beachroamer* service, operated by specially-acquired Routemasters, 527-532. No. 528 is running the final trip on the first day of the service, while Centenary car 645 waits at the Adshel.

Starr Gate Metro

Top On 9 May 2005 rebuilt Balloon 724 (in the red and yellow livery of Blackpool Transport's Metro Coastlines Line 5) waits for some low-tech track maintenance. It is standing at the green and cream Abacus shelter, which dates from 1996, when Adshel removed their shelters overnight after a disagreement with Blackpool Council.

Centre Twin-cars were rare at Starr Gate until 2003, when the entire class was pressed into Fleetwood service after double-deck cars were banned north of Thornton Gate. On 2 November 2008, the driver of 675/685 pulls away from Starr Gate terminus, dead on time with the 13.39 departure to Fleetwood.

Below 675/685 again, this time during driver-training on 23 August 2007. The livery - like 724's - is from Line 5.

- 14 -

Above Twin-car 673 in Metro Coastlines Line 11 livery on 11 July 2007.

Below 684/674, looking very smart in newly-applied Line 4 livery, leave a rather less smart turning circle on 3 July 2003.

Keeping an Eye on Things

The tramway from Starr Gate to Pleasure Beach closed for rebuilding after service on 6 September 2009. At Starr Gate, in place of the single-track circle, the double track was extended to the site of the old terminus so that cars could reverse there. The circle was retained (or rather reconstructed on a different alignment) for access to the tram wash at the side of the new depot.

In 2009 - just in time to keep an eye on the reconstruction project - the effigy of Keith Burgess, who had been head of engineering at the Pleasure Beach, was moved from the amusement park to the crazy-golf course.

Top The last few weeks of the old layout. Balloon 701's crew enjoy the Starr Gate sunshine on 13 August 2009. 701's own sunny appearance is the remains of an advertising livery, with the vinyls for the Palm Beach Hotel replaced by Metro Coastlines logos.

Second Track and wires have gone by 1 October 2009.

Third By 3 July 2010 the foundations of the new circle are in place. The spectacular but problematical new Welcome Arch has been removed for repair.

Bottom : The finished product seems to meet with approval. Flexity 008 reverses at the new terminus on 1 June 2014. The arch is still not back.

The New Depot Site

The Supertram depot stands on the site formerly occupied by a rather unprepossessing car park.

Top On 31 May 1987 Balloon 724 heads north past the deteriorating 1938 concrete fencing, inelegantly patched with lengths of angle-iron which once served as check-rail on the Fleetwood Tramroad.

Centre A panorama of the impressive new depot and its approaches under construction on 20 September 2010, before a clutter of poles, signals and security fencing spoiled the view.

Below On 13 September 2011 Standard car 147 revisited the new depot for tests, having been on display there during the Flexity launch five days earlier (*see next page*). Here it negotiates the aforesaid clutter before returning to Rigby Road.

- 17 -

Starr Gate Depot

Opposite (top) Guests at the launch of Flexity 001 on 8 September 2011, with Standard car 147 on display, as was the Western Train. (*James Millington*)

Opposite (bottom) 001 emerges from a cloud of smoke into a typical Blackpool gale on 8 September 2011, accompanied by a spectacularly ill-clad string quartet.

Top Flexity 010 receiving attention in the maintenance section of the depot on 20 March 2013.

Centre The car wash on the south side of the depot being tested by widened Balloon No. 709 on 20 December 2011.

Below During the Spring of 2014, access to Rigby Road depot was blocked by roadworks, and the heritage fleet was temporarily housed at Starr Gate, as seen here on 3 May during a visit by the Fylde Tramway Society. (*James Millington*)

The Changing Scene

Top From 1972 to 1987, the one-man cars held sway at Starr Gate, having superseded the railcoaches and Coronations. On a frigid 13 January 1979, OMO No. 13 - last to be built (in 1976) and first to be withdrawn (in 1984) - finds itself going the wrong way round the turning circle because of trackwork on New South Promenade.

Centre The OMOs were replaced by the Centenary class. Prototype 641 is running its first Sunday service on 8 July 1984, two days after making its debut.

Below Before the Centenaries were superseded by the Flexities (*opposite*), Starr Gate witnessed a very unusual vehicle - even for Blackpool. On 9 November 2011, Cardiff railgrinder No. 131, built in 1905 and borrowed from the National Tramway Museum, cleans the track before Supertram service starts in April 2012.

Who's crazy now? Arnold Palmer's golf course of 1970 is just about the oldest part of this entire scene, as Flexity 013 reverses under a watery moon on 21 November 2012. The new landscaped tracks are laid entirely in Promenade fashion – unfenced grooved rail – but just a hint of Tramroad survives in the foreground, where the toilet block is still guarded by concrete fencing and a solitary sprung gate (though not the 1965 originals).

One of Flexity 008's two guards heads for the depot, while 007 arrives from Fleetwood on 30 April 2012.

Mind the Curve

Above Standard car 159 leans into the curve after leaving the terminus in August 1965. In the right background is Squires Gate Lane.

Centre Coronation 317 - still with its original Vambac control - takes the curve on 3 September 1967. 317 was withdrawn (as 653) two years later. (*Peter Makinson*)

Bottom Brush car 631, having failed to mind the curve, is being re-railed on 20 July 1988. The circle had just been re-laid and re-wired.

Opposite (top) On 14 August 2008, Balloon 712 (in retro livery) does its best to re-create the 1960s, despite the crazy-golf course and new overhead.

Opposite (bottom) Flexity 003 whiles away the afternoon as spare car on 19 April 2012, two weeks after the Supertram service began.

Mind the Curve (2)

Above Former open-topper 241 takes the other curve - from New South Promenade into Starr Gate - on 3 September 1967. (*Peter Makinson*)

Centre In 1978/79 the paved reservation was cut back so that the change from grooved to bullhead rail took place on straight track. The inner rails on both tracks were fitted with check rails to discourage derailments. On 9 April 1984, OMO car 9 was allowed over the inner curve whilst the check-rail was removed for replacement, and duly de-railed. By the time this picture was taken, No. 9 had been dragged sideways, using the time-honoured greasy plates, but promptly fell off the other side. Note the altered overhead.

Bottom Towing car 680 passes what looks like a builder's yard during construction of a new sea-wall and Promenade on 2 May 1998. Completely new overhead this time.

- 24 -

Mind the Curve (2)

Right Balloon 719 needs a bit of help to get round on 27 June 1987. 719 had just received 1980s-style green and cream after carrying advertising liveries since 1981. The car remains at Blackpool as part of the reserve 'B Fleet' *(see page 120)*.

Below Flexity 008 glides effortlessly round on 11 July 2013. The entrance to the Starr Gate depot complex is on the left.

From Footpath to Headshunt

Left Looking up New South Promenade on 9 April 1984, with Permanent Way gang car 624 standing by while workmen renew the check-rail on the curve.

Below The new depot head-shunt - formerly the footpath - was used to unload the 16 Flexity cars after their 1,000-mile road journey from Bombardier's historic works at Bautzen near Dresden. On 16 March 2012 a Bombardier engineer drives 010 from the low-loader into the depot, while 008 passes on driver training.

2. New South Promenade

New South Promenade was built between 1922 and 1926, extending the sea-wall, Promenade and tramway from Pleasure Beach to the borough boundary at Starr Gate. It was designed by John C. Robinson - Blackpool's Borough Architect from 1920 to 1944 - who was responsible for much of the architectural backdrop to the Promenade tramway, as well as the surviving Tramroad stations at Bispham and Little Bispham.

Above : Balloon 717 - with a rather tired, end-of-season look - stops to pick up northbound passengers at the Star Hotel on 5 September 2009, a day before the New South Promenade tramway closed for rebuilding. 723 heads for Starr Gate.

The South End

Above No. 328, the last of 25 Coronation cars, was 13 years old when photographed – slightly battle-scarred – at the south end of the Promenade on 3 September 1967, and ran for another four years. (*Peter Makinson*)

Below One of several classical allusions by J.C. Robinson on New South Promenade was this pair of sphinxes, casting stony eyes on OMO 2 as it chases No. 9 towards Abercorn Place stop on 19 August 1979.

Abercorn Place

Top Abercorn Place was still undeveloped when the driver of this Circular Tour Boat car checked for traffic, before turning off the Promenade onto the street track. When the Tour was revived in 1957, the southbound junction was fitted with new points, and the northbound junction removed. (*Malcolm King collection*)

Centre Even in 1962 - when Boat car 231 was approaching Abercorn Place from Starr Gate - New South Promenade was still not completely built up. The crescent between Cardigan Place and Abercorn Place - left unfinished in 1935 - had just been filled with flats, but the final block remained empty until 1964/65. Buildings might be few, but tram stops were prolific, literally one at every street corner - seven in all on New South Promenade, where today there are just two.

Below Balloon 724 leaves Abercorn Place on 31 May 1987, with 701 approaching. In December 1986 experimental Parafil span wiring was strung from galvanised poles on the west of the line between Abercorn Place and Harrow Place. This survived until the overhead on the entire system was replaced in 1996.

– 29 –

Abercorn Place

Above On 18 January 1986 new rails are being unloaded near Abercorn Place by rail-crane 751 (formerly Brush car 628) propelled by sister car 623. (*Peter Fitton*)

Centre While Starr Gate turning circle was relaid early in 1988, the service was cut back to Abercorn Place. Trams showed *Harrowside* on the blind, running single line from there, as with Centenary 643 on 5 April.

Bottom 21st-century Abercorn Place, with new overhead wiring and new sea-wall. A lone passenger boards Balloon 713 on 4 April 2008, its first day out in Metro Coastlines Line 7 livery.

Opposite (top) OMO car 3 leaves Abercorn Place on 25 January 1979, running wrong-line because of track-work on New South Promenade.

Opposite (bottom) Flexity 002 repeats the process on 1 March 2012 during driver training. Nothing at all survives from the previous view.

The next stop after Abercorn Place was Harrow Place. An intermediate stop at Cardigan Place (sometimes referred to as Jubilee Hotel) disappeared in 1971.

Harrow Place

Above Brush car 292 or 293 - the only two still with Vs and sweeps - approaches Harrow Place on 18 March 1961. The Parisian-style lamps (first used at Blackpool in 1893) are being replaced by fluorescent tubes.

Below Restored twin-car T2/272 in much the same location on 2 May 2014. The 20 ft. mirror-ball, erected in 2002, was said to be the largest in the world, with 47,000 mirrors.

Harrow Place

Above OMO car 7, abandoned at Harrow Place on 15 December 1981. No. 7 spent three nights on the Promenade after becoming stuck in snow near Abercorn Place late on 13 December.

Centre On 4 September 1998, Balloon 718 leaves a temporary Harrow Place tram stop. The remains of J.C. Robinson's Promenade are piled high to be re-cycled as hard core for the new sea-wall.

Bottom Centenary car 642 pulls away from the northbound stop on 16 February 2006. The southbound stop was two poles further north.

Harrow Place

Top OMO 8 travelling north wrong-line from Harrow Place on 16 December 1978.

Centre Coronation 660 leaves Harrow Place on 24 October 2007 against a backdrop of lesser mirror-balls. The Solarium on the right was another J.C. Robinson creation.

Below Work on the Supertram platforms had only just started when Balloon 717 carried guests to the Flexity launch at Starr Gate depot on 8 September 2011.

Opposite (top) The view from northbound Flexity No. 012 as it approaches the shelter on 27 April 2012 – its second day in service – with 003 just arriving.

Opposite (bottom) On 11 August 2012, southbound Flexity 005 leaves Harrow Place while 009 is ready to depart.

Harrowside

Harrowside tram stop is - or was - opposite the north end of the Solarium. Harrowside once served as the terminus of the Promenade route, though only during the winter of 1932/33. Cars ran single-line south of Burlington Road crossover to Harrowside, which was then the end of the buildings - mostly private hotels - along New South Promenade.

In following winters the Promenade service ran through to Starr Gate, and Harrowside didn't re-appear as a destination until August 1950, when Burlington Road crossover was replaced by one at Harrowside. In the 1950s and early 1960s extra services (i.e. timetabled, but not publicly) sometimes ran to Harrowside.

Above At Christmas 1965 a Harrowside - Bispham service is being operated by Coronations, two of which are reversing on a foggy day.

Below Harrowside crossover was re-laid in 1979. OMO car 3 is running single-track between Pleasure Beach and Starr Gate on 13 January.

Harrowside

Above OMO car 2 passes the boating pool, the crossover (being re-laid) and another of J.C. Robinson's classical extravaganzas on 26 January 1979.

Centre Heavy vehicles travelling over the Promenade tracks gradually reduced the concrete slabs to the consistency of crazy paving. After the new sea-wall was completed, the track between Pleasure Beach and Harrowside was completely re-paved early in 2004. Towing car 679 passes the shelter on 24 March. In the background the Solarium is being transformed into the Solaris Centre.

Bottom The first articulated tram to run in Blackpool was this *Roadliner* prototype, which was tested spasmodically from June 2000 until it was damaged by fire in January 2007. The row of Chrysler PT Cruisers is part of the Totally Transport vehicle rally on 25 June 2006.

Harrowside

For many years there were no tram shelters at all between Starr Gate and Manchester Square, but after cars began turning at Harrowside, a 'temporary' steel shelter was erected there in 1951.

Top Brush car 632 departs from Harrowside on 25 March 1986.

Centre The temporary shelter saw the Coronations come and go, and nearly outlasted the OMOs which followed. On 14 August 1985 the shelter welcomed new Centenary car 651 - or at least almost new; this was its first day out following several weeks' absence since entering service on 16 July. After a few more fitful appearances, 651 disappeared again until January 1987.

Below The steel shelter at Harrowside was replaced in August 1988 by a standard - but remarkably camera-shy - Adshel, which can just be seen in the distance as Brush car 634 passes two Routemasters on 4 June 1989.

Above The Adshel was followed in 1997 by an equally reclusive Abacus shelter, which lasted only a year before being displaced by Promenade reconstruction and re-erected at Central Pier. Later Harrowside received a second Abacus, seen here on 6 May 2001, with Stockport 5.

Below The second Abacus was moved again, but only a few feet this time, away from the sloping footpath. Lest this book give the impression that New South Promenade's climate alternated between sunshine and snow, rebuilt Balloon 708 picks up a few passengers on a showery 4 September 2009, two days before Harrowside disappeared from the tramway map.

Burlington Road West

Above The first stop after Harrowside was once at Wimbourne Place (also known as Southdown) but this disappeared in 1971. Then came Burlington Road West, as it was known to distinguish it from the Burlington Road stop on Lytham Road. After the Squires Gate route closed in 1961, the West rather fell out of use, only to be reinstated in 2012 for the Supertram stop. Flexity 002 on New Year's Eve, 2013. Unusually the platforms are staggered.

Below OMO 6 approaches Burlington Road stop on 26 January 1979.

Burlington Road West

Top When the Promenade was rebuilt between 1998 and 2000, Blackpool Council indulged in some optimistic landscaping, including this swathe of daffodils, toning nicely with Jubilee 762 as it approaches Burlington Road on 10 April 2001. The daffodils didn't last long but 762 survived until the end of the old tramway in November 2011, and is now preserved by the National Tramway Museum at Crich.

Centre During the winter of 2008/9, the tramway operated only between Pleasure Beach and Little Bispham. However from 29 January to late March, Brush car 636 used New South Promenade to test a new bogie. 636 passes the bagged-up Burlington Road stop on 10 February 2009.

Bottom On 1 November 2011, a week before it left for Crich, 762 made its only run over the rebuilt (but unopened) New South Promenade tramway, carrying NTM representatives on a farewell trip. Here it leaves Burlington Road West, in almost the same spot as the top picture. (*James Millington*)

Above Coronation 660 draws up at the old northbound stop on 24 October 2007.

Burlington Road West

Below Once the new track on New South Promenade was completed, the overhead line crews set about adjusting the overhead for the wider spacing of the tracks. Powered by its diesel engine, car 754 has reached Burlington Road West on 3 December 2010, accompanied by Unimog tower wagon 939 and the mess bus, Metrorider 512. Beyond 512 is the new northbound platform.

Star Hotel

Above There weren't usually enough passengers at the southbound Star Hotel stop to justify the *Q Here* sign. OMO 11 loads (slowly) on Easter Sunday, 26 March 1978. Rising in the background is the Space Tower (1974).

Star Hotel

Below The scene had changed significantly by 25 April 2004, when Brush car 637 called at the northbound stop. The Space Tower went to Morecambe in 1992, the *Big One* roller-coaster opened in 1994 and the new Promenade in 2000.

Previous page The *Big One* justifies its label, dwarfing the Star Hotel and towing car 680, as it takes shape on 19 December 1993. *(Peter Fitton)*

Star Hotel

The Star Hotel stop - like those at Abercorn Place and Harrowside - was a casualty of the Supertram system, and was used for the last time on 6 September 2009. When the New South Promenade tramway reopened on 4 April 2012, the only stops were at Harrow Place and Burlington Road West.

Top On Monday morning, 7 September 2009, Inspector Gill Hall bags up the southbound Star Hotel stop, never to be used again. The line on New South Promenade had closed for rebuilding the previous night.

Below Under the eye of the watchful Gatso, Cardiff works car 131 (on loan from the National Tramway Museum, and operated by their staff) heads towards the Star Hotel at a sedate 8 m.p.h., whilst scrubbing the new rails on 9 November 2011. The barriers near the car park entrance delineate 131's field of operations. Blackpool had its own rail-grinder until November 2008, when No. 752 went to Heaton Park for preservation.

Ocean Boulevard

After the Star Hotel there was an unusually long gap – some 700 yards – to the next stop at Pleasure Beach, the intermediate stop at Watson Road having been a victim of wartime cuts in 1942 and never reinstated. The backdrop to this stretch of tramway changed considerably in the early 1990s.

Above Experimental Centenary car 651 in original livery passes the Pleasure Beach monorail (*see page 62*) on 13 December 1987.

Centre The monorail lost pride of place when the row of shops known as *Ocean Boulevard* was built in stages between 1989 and 1991. Car 641 passes in June 1993, in the second and last version of green and cream worn by the class.

Bottom Ocean Boulevard had only a few seasons in the limelight before it in turn was overshadowed by *The Big One*, here being erected on 20 February 1994. A new look, too, for Centenary 642, advertising Regal cigarettes in the days when such things were permitted. (*Peter Fitton*)

3. Pleasure Beach
The Turning Circle

The turning circle at Pleasure Beach opened on 26 March 1937, eighteen months before the Starr Gate circle, and just in time for Easter. To cope with the enormous traffic generated by the Pleasure Beach, the circle was double track, which allowed cars to reverse in either direction.

Above Towing car 680 - once the front half of twin-car 280/T10 - rounds the circle anti-clockwise on 15 April 1979.

The South Curve

From 1937 until 1971, cars arriving at Pleasure Beach from the south used a single-track curve to reach the northbound stop on the outer circle. Thereafter the curve was only used in emergencies.

Top Glasgow 1297 is tested with a pantograph on 9 April 1984, but its bogies were too close together to follow the prescribed line; a week later 1297 received a trolley pole.

Centre On 20 April 1984, Balloon 724 derailed, blocking the northbound main line and the curve onto the outer circle. As the inner circle was being relaid, southbound cars had to run down to Harrowside or Starr Gate, and northbound cars - as with OMO 6 - had to use the south curve and outer circle in the old manner.

Below The curve was used for the last time during a private tour on 4 November 2007. Centenary car 647 and Fleetwood Box 40 eye each other under suitably sombre skies.

Round the Circle

The Pleasure Beach circle was a fascinating place to watch the trams, as they pirouetted round each other in ever-changing combinations.

Above An ensemble of twin-cars - surprisingly attractive vehicles, despite being basically a Coronation front-end stuck on a railcoach body. 675/685 is followed by 687/677 on 27 July 1997.

Below On 26 August 1982, Brush car 633 - the Post Office tram, complete with counter and post-box - turns onto the outer circle, while 704 and 710 reverse on the inner.

The Outer Circle Stop

For many years there were two northbound stops at Pleasure Beach – one on the main line and another on the outer circle. Until 1971 cars from Starr Gate took the south-to-west curve and loaded on the outer circle. Cars starting at Pleasure Beach generally reversed on the inner circle and loaded on the main line. It was all rather confusing for passengers, as cars to the same destination could be loading at either stop.

Left Trailer car T10 – just six months old – loads at the outer circle stop in July 1961 for another run to Little Bispham behind towing-car 280. This was the standard itinerary for twin-cars, with occasional trips to Fleetwood and Starr Gate, these being the only places they could turn round. Seven twin-cars were made double-ended in the 1960s, but T10 was not among them, being withdrawn (as 690) in 1972.

Below A Brush car loads on a wet night during the 1965 Illuminations. The poster above the tram stop sign reads *Special 12-Mile Tour of the Illuminations by Tramcar.*

The Outer Circle Stop

Above Confusingly the two northbound stops each proclaim *All Cars Stop Here* - Blackpool Transport's standard wording for a compulsory stop. A board by the outer-circle stop says - rather more circumspectly - *Cars leave here - all stops to North Pier, Bispham, Fleetwood.* Balloon 707 is followed by Brush car 621 on 6 August 1970. (*David Christie*)

Centre In 1971, through cars were transferred from the outer circle to the main line. The outer circle stop remained, but was moved one pole west. It's not clear how much the stop was used in the mid-1970s, but photographs towards the end of the decade usually show it bagged up and out of use. The stop was still there - un-bagged this time - when Dreadnought 59 called on 23 May 1982, but had been removed altogether by August that year.

Bottom For some years the outer circle stop was also used as a loading point for Illuminations Tours, and a large wooden sign was attached to the pole each Autumn. This applied even after the normal stop sign had gone, as here with 701 on 1 October 1983, but 1984 seems to have been the last year.

Outer Circle Ghost Stop

The removal of the official tram stop on the outer circle in the summer of 1982 didn't alter the need for cars reversing in a clockwise direction to load somewhere. So the original pre-1972 loading point near the junction continued to serve a useful purpose - tram stop or no tram stop.

Top Boat 606 loads at the unofficial stop on a balmy August evening in 1982. There could be tears, as someone has just lost their prize from the Pleasure Beach.

Centre An enterprising inspector has taken advantage of 722's off-side doors to divert the queue from the main-line stop on 26 May 1986.

Below Balloon 711 loads at the unofficial outer circle stop in August 1988, while No. 723 prepares to go anti-clockwise.

Winter Manoeuvres

Top The turning circle was usually left to rust during the winter, but while the track at Harrowside was being relaid in the winter of 1978/79, southbound cars reversed round the circle. This is OMO 9 going anti-clockwise on 26 January 1979.

Centre The inspector then swings No. 9's trolley while the driver changes ends. On the left is the unloading stop (*see page 76*).

Below Once the inspector has handed the single-line staff - the 'square rolling-pin' - to the driver, No. 9 heads off to Starr Gate wrong-line or 'bang-road,' to use the old railway term in common currency at Blackpool. This was the so-called Winter of Discontent, with local authority workers on strike - hence the untreated roadway.

Relaying the Circle

The turning circle, which had previously been laid in paved bullhead rail (standard railway section 85R, as used on the Fleetwood Tramroad) was relaid with normal grooved tramway rail in 1984 - the inner circle in April/May, and the outer circle in November/December.

Top On 29 April, Brush car 626 negotiates the outer track. In the background the future Sandcastle is little more than that, with the remains of the Open-air Bath awaiting recycling.

Centre On 20 April, Balloon 720 loads at the 'ghost stop' (*see page 52*).

Below New rails being unloaded from crane car 751 (628), pushed by PW car 624 on 17 April 1984. (*Peter Fitton*)

Above The relaying altered the appearance of the turning circle, as the tracks were surfaced in mass concrete rather than Blackpool's traditional paving flags. The west side of the circle had always been protected by a Tramroad-style concrete fence, though the rest of the Promenade line managed well enough without. By 1984 *anno domini* and derailments had taken their toll, and during the relaying a new style of fence was erected. Unfortunately the garden within the circle was left in a deplorable state, minus most of its wrought-iron fencework. The traction poles, too, were no credit to anybody. Centenary car 651 negotiates the inner circle on 8 February 1986, whilst the service was cut back to Pleasure Beach by trackwork on New South Promenade.

Below In August 1988, Balloon 708 passes through the sea-defence wall which was part of the 1984 work. At high tides, temporary barriers were slotted into place across the tram tracks.

The Inspector's Cabin

In 1961 the Transport Department built a wooden cabin for the inspectors, just inside the circle.

Above The hut wasn't normally used in winter, but on 1 February 1986, OMO car 10 is reversing at Pleasure Beach during trackwork on New South Promenade.

Opposite (top) Inspector's view of Boat 600 at the short-lived heritage stop (*see page 92*) on 27 May 2012.

Opposite (bottom) In May 2013 the cabin - now the oldest tramway feature at the Pleasure Beach - was dressed overall for the heritage operation. On 8 June, Flexity 005 heads north, while Brush car 627 - decorated for the Queen's Diamond Jubilee - heads nowhere.

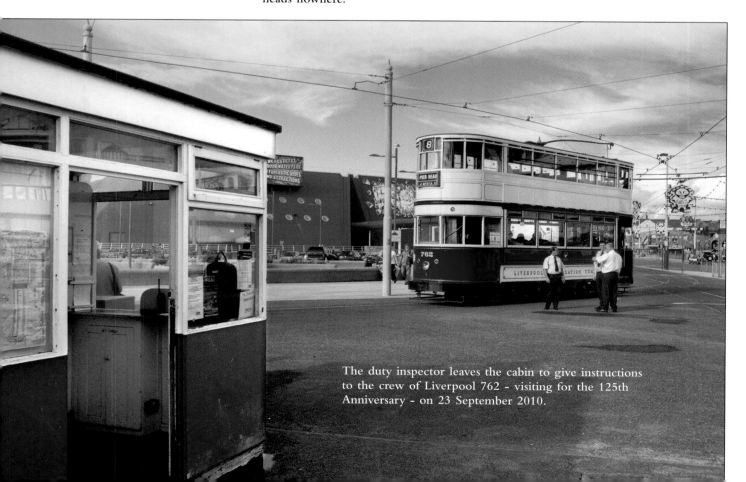

The duty inspector leaves the cabin to give instructions to the crew of Liverpool 762 - visiting for the 125th Anniversary - on 23 September 2010.

Sign Language

To avoid having to leave their comfortable cabin, the inspectors evolved a sign language to give the crews of 'specials' their next destination:

Bispham – banging clenched fists one on top of the other.

Depot – arms crossed over the chest with the hands outstretched to make an 'X' shape.

Tower – hands together pointing upwards as if in prayer.

Talbot Square – top hand horizontal, lower hand vertical to make a 'T' shape.

Break – like holding a piece of wood and breaking it.

Cabin – thumb and first finger form a small letter 'c'.

Little Bispham – Cabin gesture (to mean Little) followed by Bispham one.

Cleveleys – as for Cabin but with thumb and finger spread wider to form a large 'C'.

Fleetwood – pinch of the nose (for the smell of fish).

From ex-guards Peter Makinson and Paul Turner.

New-look Circle

Top After New South Promenade was rebuilt in 2000, work continued north-wards, including a new sea-wall by the turning circle. Threading its way through the building site on 23 March 2004 is towing car 679.

Centre Centenary 643 is held up by Unimog tower wagon 940 on 2 May 2005, while 147 and Fleetwood Box car 40 reverse on the inner circle.

Below A motorist's view of the new-look turning circle on 31 July 2007, taken from the car-park access road which was built alongside the tramway in 2003/4. Boat car 604 is followed round the outer circle by twin-car 684/674.

Opposite (top) In 2007 the centre of the circle was landscaped, providing a vantage point to photograph the *Hot Ice* skaters, promoting their show (and tram) on 29 August 2007. Behind 721 is 719, also advertising the Pleasure Beach.

Opposite (below) Coronation 660 negotiates the circle on 29 September 2007.

One-way Circle

Once the 2007 season ended on 4 November, the entire tramway closed down for the winter to facilitate reconstruction. After sixty seasons' service, the main line and turning circle were completely reconstructed, replacing the two-way double-track circle by a one-way (anti-clockwise) circuit, though with double track round most of it.

Top On 18 March 2008, Brush car 622 passes the site of the old south curve during a test run round the circle, the paving as yet unblemished by use.

Centre Next day Centenary car 646 served as test car.

Bottom The one-way two-track circle introduced a new hazard; on 1 November 2010 OMO 8's driver checks for over-taking - or perhaps under-taking - trams before setting off. Note the right-hand controls.

Above Stockport 5 with Bolton 66 on 28 October 2009. A shortage of cars has pressed the little four-wheeler into emergency use during the busy half-term week.

Below The new Flexity cars are relatively rare users of the Pleasure Beach circle, but 003 reverses there during driver training on 9 August 2012.

A Monorail Diversion

A brief diversion from trams on the Promenade was provided by the Pleasure Beach monorail, which from May 1966 until November 2012 operated on a mile-long route, running parallel with the tramway between the Star Hotel and Pleasure Beach stops.

The monorail was originally designed by the Swiss firm of Von Roll for the 1964 Exposition at Lausanne. When the fair closed, some of the cars and equipment were bought by the Pleasure Beach; the rest went to the Montreal Exposition of 1967, and some are still running on that site.

The line had three stations at various times – originally North and Central, later Central and South, but usually just Central. There were four trains – one open, one closed and two semi-open. In the early years two or three ran simultaneously, but latterly only one.

Above The enclosed train, known as the *Pullman*, soars over the amusement park on 28 June 1967, just about to turn right towards Central Station. The 25 ft. Gulliver was inspired by a giant figure at Lausanne. (*Geoffrey Tribe*)

Centre The two semi-open trains were known in Blackpool as *Lausanne A* and *Lausanne B*. One of them approaches North Station in 1967. This station closed in 1977 and the line was diverted round the Casino building.

Bottom The open train, known as the *Miner*, was initially painted grey. In this rare 1967 view of two trains on the line, the *Miner* has emerged from the depot, while a *Lausanne* waits on the main line.

Pleasure Beach Monorail

Top The *Miner* - now red and yellow - passes the cable-car station (since closed) on 19 July 1997.

Centre On 8 June 2004 *Lausanne B* encountered a problem soon after leaving Central Station. The driver stopped on the only ground-level section to unload the passengers, who seem to be viewing their predicament with mixed emotions. Originally it was intended to build a station at this point. (*Alan Robson*)

Below By 24 November 2011 the fleet had been reduced to three, the *Miner* having been broken up. All three survivors are visible, with *Lausanne A* and *Lausanne B* (blue), flanking the unserviceable *Pullman*. The board on the left suggests that the *Pullman* hadn't run since 2010, and indeed may not have run again before the line closed.

- 63 -

4. Pleasure Beach

The Main Line

Above OMO car 3, newly fitted with an experimental Brecknell Willis pantograph, passes over the north junction on 21 April 1979. On the right is the Grade II-listed Casino building - almost contemporary with the turning circle, having been opened in May 1939. The paving of the tram track is the usual Blackpool hotchpotch of flagstones, tarmacadam and concrete.

South Junction

Above The south junction on Bank Holiday Monday, 3 May 2004, with the main line occupied by first-series Balloons in three varieties - left to right, Nos. 707, 701 and 706.

Below Pantograph car 167 - loaned for the Centenary by the National Tramway Museum and rather messed up by its sponsors, ICI - turns onto the south junction in October 1985.

South Junction

Top Brush car 634 heads across the south junction for Starr Gate on 23 May 1982. No. 634 carried this cheerful advertising livery for Blackpool Zoo from 1981 to 1983 after the original Zoo tram, No. 622, had been damaged in an accident.

Centre There wasn't much scope for variety at the south junction, but No. 700 has concocted a fairly unfathomable manoeuvre on 29 December 2000, in unaccustomed weather for Balloons. (*Peter Fitton*)

Below Not easy to get south-facing views of the junction in sunshine, but Brush car 627's pointed front makes it just possible in the early morning of 27 September 2003. In the background are the remains of the Promenade shelter which stood by the south curve.

The Main Line

Above Trams, monorail and funfair - a picture which perhaps encapsulates the appeal of the Pleasure Beach as a tramway location. *H.M.S. Blackpool* tucks neatly behind Brush car 621 on 21 April 1981. The Eli Wheels in the background were contemporaries of the turning circle, being built by the Eli Bridge Co. of Illinois in 1936 and 1938 (and removed in 1984).

Below This January 1980 view shows several long-established Pleasure Beach features - the open-air baths, the remains of the siding (*see page 70*), the inspector's cabin (*see page 56*), the Casino and the chain fencing. Tower wagon 240 (bought from Manchester when their trolleybus system closed in 1966) has been demoted to support a flagging traction standard, while its replacement, No. 443, occupies the southbound track alongside OMO 10 on the Fleetwood service.

The Main Line

Above The main line in winter. Standard 40 dwarfs conduit car 4 during a farewell tour on 30 November 1985, before both cars returned to the National Tramway Museum. (*Peter Fitton*)

Below The main line in summer. On Sunday 7 August 1983, Balloon 709 loads at the stop, while 713 heads for Starr Gate. On the inner circle, Balloon 703 is causing a twin-car to block the north junction.

The New Main Line

Top The main line was relaid - minus crossover - along with the circle during the winter of 2007/08. On a gloomy 10 October 2011, the overhead crew on tower wagon No. 939 check the pantographs of passing trams, in this case Brush car 632, admirably restored to 1970s condition, complete with illuminated advertising boxes.

Centre In early 2012, driver training went on at the northern end of the tramway whilst final remedial work was under way on the southern parts of the line. Flexity 005 - without numbers or vinyls - is escorted through a security fence at Pleasure Beach on 5 January 2012. (*James Millington*)

Below On 2 June 2012 Flexity 014, just two weeks old, pauses at the warning signal - and the short-lived heritage stop - outside the inspector's cabin. The original curve of the line here has been replaced by a curious stretch of straight track, as if to allow for a platform.

The Siding

The 1937 layout at Pleasure Beach incorporated a siding off the northbound main line. Though little used, it remained connected and wired at both ends till the late 1950s, when a concrete crush barrier was built over the northern exit.

Top Coronation 317 has been shunted onto the siding on 17 August 1958. (*David Packer*)

Centre Perhaps the only time a Pantograph car ever used the siding. During the 75th Anniversary celebrations on 29 September 1960, No. 170 from Bispham Depot awaits the arrival of cars from Rigby Road, so that the morning procession can form in the correct order. On the right is General Manager Joseph Franklin with the Traffic Department management.

Below The southern end of the siding remained connected, and was used for parking casualties, like Standard 160 (minus trolley head) in August 1961. Sister car 49 arrives amidst a fine display of early Sixties fashions. The last known use of the siding was by the illuminated *Rocket* on the opening night of the 1972 Lights. It was disconnected in 1973/74 but some of the track remained until 1999.

Main Line Stop

Top A July 1961 view of the main-line stop, looking much as it had for years, apart from the concrete fence erected over the north end of the siding in the late 1950s. The poles and chains date from at least the 1920s. The nearer Balloon is No. 246.

Centre On 23 July 1966 three empty Boats, headed by 225 and followed by an illuminated Standard car, wait at the main-line stop during their lunch break. The inspector's cabin has a notice directing passengers for North Pier, Bispham and Fleetwood to the outer-circle stop. The overhead on the siding is still complete.

Below In 1971, when cars from Starr Gate began using the main line, the layout of the stop was changed so that the queue faced south instead of north. The original Zoo tram - Brush car 622 - loads at Easter 1978. The wiring on the siding has been cut back and a 1972-style stop sign has replaced the old roundel.

- 71 -

Main Line Stop

Above Evening sunshine allows a southward view, with new Jubilee car 762 loading at a litter-strewn stop in June 1982. Pole 87 has a 1972-style hand-painted sign as well as the new 1982-style sign with Brush car.

Below A close-up of the loading arrangements on an August evening in 1982. OMO car 10 had just been repainted in an economy style, with two crests instead of four, and the fleet number on the side of the cab. It was not repeated.

Main Line Stop

Top The south-facing queue (which replaced the north-facing arrangement in 1971) could cause problems at busy times. In September 1982 twin-car 683/673, with 114 seats, will soon clear the crowds, but only after edging its way through the lengthening queue to reverse on the inner circle.

Centre In 1984 the old northward-facing queue was restored. On 25 July that year the duty inspector leaves his cabin to supervise the loading of Brush car 627.

Below A general view of the new arrangement on the same summer evening, with OMO car 1 showing off its new green and cream livery. The lettering on the pavement by the stop reads *Queue Here for All Trams.*

- 73 -

A Shelter at last

Above The north-facing queue only lasted for a few months, as in August 1984 the Pleasure Beach was finally blessed with a tram shelter. A large non-standard Adshel was erected at the main-line stop, adorned with a comprehensive list of destinations. Visiting Manchester car 765 loads on the evening of 30 July 1985.

Below The other end of the shelter is seen at Easter 1988, with Balloon 724 in a new livery - in effect the 1950s scheme without the thin green band across the cab. The livery was altered in January 1989 to incorporate a thick green band below the windscreens. Centenary car 643 in the distance.

Pleasure Beach Interchange

Above The new shelter at night, with Jubilee 761 waiting hopefully for passengers on 19 January 1986. The tram service had been cut back to Pleasure Beach during track relaying near Harrowside.

Centre A connecting bus service was run to Starr Gate. On 9 February 1986, OMO car 8 turns onto the circle after exchanging passengers with AEC Swift 591. Passengers seem to be in short supply, but New South Promenade was rarely busy in winter.

Bottom Dennis Lancet 598 waits for the next southbound car, having transferred its northbound passengers – if any – onto OMO car 10.

In 1971, when through cars began using the main line instead of the outer circle, a separate unloading stop was provided for northbound passengers. There are surprisingly few pictures of this stop, and even less of passengers unloading. Not many did, of course.

Unloading Stop

Above The unloading stop was attached to Pole No. 84, which had once carried the frog for the siding. Fortuitously the stop (and bamboo pole) just appear in this view on 24 February 1979 of OMO 2, hinting at an exotic destination.

Below A better idea of the stop's location can be gleaned from this picture of OMO 11 - apparently intent on re-occupying the siding - on 10 October 1981. (*Peter Makinson*)

Unloading Stop

Above For the 1986 season, the unloading stop was moved twenty yards north to Pole 85. In an unusual winter pairing on 8 March 1986, experimental Centenary car 651 is about to pass Dreadnought 59, on filming duty for the BBC.

Centre Blackpool's visitors easily become confused, and *Unloading Only* was sometimes beyond them. After countless instances of people queuing at unloading stops here and elsewhere, this enigmatic blue diamond was introduced across the system in 1996. Brush car 622 - colour co-ordinated - passes on 10 May 2007.

Bottom If pictures of the unloading stop are rare, this combination is even more so. Balloon 713 is wearing the most ephemeral advertising livery ever seen in Blackpool, lasting just 13 days for the Conservative Party conference in 2007. 713's run to Little Bispham on 2 October was designed to serve the conference hotels.

The Crossover

When the crossover at Dean Street *(see page 105)* was deemed to be worn out, it was decided to replace it by one at Pleasure Beach. Work began at the end of the 1986 season.

Top Swathed against bitter weather in January 1987, the permanent-way gang replace the southbound track, with works car 624 in attendance.

Centre The overhead line gang, with Unimog tower-wagon 440, get ready to string the wire for the crossover on 19 February. The new Sandcastle centre is in the background.

Below Towing car 678 uses the crossover on 21 June 1987, seemingly without turning the trolley, which can't have impressed the inspector.

Plus ça change

These three photographs were taken over a forty-year period in the same place - opposite the entrance to the Pleasure Beach. Less obviously they are all of the same tram.

Top On 30 May 1970, railcoach 619 - once 282 - heads past the Casino towards the south junction to reverse on the outer circle. (*Geoffrey Tribe*)

Centre 619 is back outside the Casino on 6 June 1976, but this time heading north as OMO car 7, newly repainted in red and cream after wearing yellow and crimson since 1973.

Bottom Once more on the main line outside the Casino, on 19 September 2009, but now 619 again, having been rebuilt as a *faux* Fleetwood Tramroad Vanguard car in 1987. Although 619 is on the main line, this track had not been in regular use since the line to Starr Gate closed on 6 September 2009 for reconstruction. Thereafter all cars used the circle, leaving the southbound main line (and a short stretch of the northbound) out of use. During the 2009 Illuminations the disused tracks were used - as here - to stack spare cars.

Car 282/619/7 retired a few weeks after the last picture was taken, and is now running on the Heaton Park tramway.

North Junction

Above : Boat car 605's guard changes the points at the north junction in July 1981. Behind is Balloon 719 in an advertising livery for the Blackpool Tower company.

Below Some dire-looking paving on 30 July 1985, as Brush car 636 - the last with roof windows - turns onto the inner circle. 622 is loading at the new northbound shelter (*see page 74*).

Learning
the Ropes

Above ... or in Blackpool's case, the bamboo pole. Trainee conductors learn the delicate art of trolleying, with Balloon 700 at the north junction on 23 May 2001.

Centre That's a pantograph ... Centenary car 646 (in all-over white between advertising liveries) does the honours for the same group of trainees.

Bottom ... and these are points. High-visibility vests have replaced orange shirts by 19 May 2006. Behind Boat 602 is the Illuminations Department's much-admired Thunderbirds rocket (*see also page 169*) which was auctioned off in 2008.

The Stop Moves North

Above The Adshel erected at the main-line stop in August 1984 served until the start of the summer service on 18 May 1992, when new - or rather old - loading arrangements were introduced. All cars loaded at a resurrected outer circle stop, including those from Starr Gate, which once more used the south-to-west curve. This system was abandoned after only a day, in favour of service cars loading on the main line, and specials on the outer circle. In this June 1992 picture, Boat 606 loads at the old stop, while 719 has just left the shelter.

Below The new arrangement re-introduced the old problem that passengers didn't know which stop to use, and lasted only a few weeks before both northbound stops were replaced by a makeshift one north of the junction (though the stop returned to the shelter for the winter). This gimcrack arrangement also applied in 1993, when Boat 605 loaded in June at what one correspondent to the *Gazette* described as 'a cattle pen'.

The Stop Moves North

Top The new stop remained unsatisfactory and unsheltered until an Abacus - Blackpool's new standard shelter with attractive green and cream fluting - was erected in June 1996. Replica Vanguard 619 leaves for Cabin on 21 September 1997.

Centre The old stop and shelter on the main line remained in place, although closed off in summer. In July 1992 twin-car 674/684 passes on its way to the new stop. The perils of contracting out the advertising are illustrated by these posters from the local taxi association. The shelter disappeared in March 1996, along with sixty other Adshels around the town.

Below Jubilee 762 loads at Easter 1999, on its re-entry into service after a major rebuild. 762 carried this superb livery for just two seasons.

The Northbound Stop

Above The Abacus shelter was removed at the end of 2007. For the 2008 season the northbound stop was once more without a shelter. Boat 600 loads on 27 September 2008, having been named *Duchess of Cornwall* by H.R.H. herself three months earlier. The strings of bulbs - once standard on the Boats - were newly re-fitted.

Centre The pole was adorned with this curious sign, like a bus stop gone wrong. Brush car 623 loads on 26 May 2008 in the wartime livery which it carried from 2007 until withdrawn in 2009 for preservation at Heaton Park.

Bottom On 31 May 2008, passengers could choose between a helicopter at £25 for a five-minute return trip to the Tower, or a Standard car for rather less. No. 147's driver waits for custom.

Trueform with Twin-cars

Above His Master's Tram? No – just looking, it seems, as Metro-liveried twin-car 673/683 loads at dusk on 29 October 2009. This Trueform Elite shelter – the new standard for the upgraded tramway – was erected at the northbound stop in November 2008 and removed at the beginning of September 2011. The southern face of the stop sign now reads *Queue Here*.

Below Father struggles with push-chair, while offspring struggles aboard trailer 682 on 21 October 2010. The low-floor revolution is still eighteen months away.

Pointwork Puzzles

Opposite (top) Pointwork maintenance used to be a pretty basic affair. Balloon 700 waits for the north junction points to be sorted out on 20 August 2007.

Opposite (bottom) Supertram points involve mobile phones, much puzzlement, even - as a last resort - recourse to the manual. If all else fails, the traditional point-bar can still be used.

Above Unfortunately things weren't so simple on 27 July 2012, when Flexity 005 was directed to turn at Pleasure Beach - a rare manoeuvre these days. 005's guard applies the point-iron in time-honoured fashion - but to no avail.

Centre Men - they're useless. 005's second guard tries feminine subtlety, but with no more success.

Bottom This isn't woman's work. 005's driver applies some real brute force. All to no avail, however, and the circle proved inaccessible for several days, causing the weekend's heritage service to be abandoned.

Southbound Stop

Top Standard car 160 unloads in July 1965, when queues of trams were an everyday sight.

Centre Centenary 651 transfers its few passengers onto AEC Swift No. 576 on 8 February 1986, whilst New South Promenade is relaid.

Below Standard 147 leaves the stop at dusk, working a rather premature Santa Special on 15 November 2008.

Opposite (top) Clipboard in hand, the inspector waits at the stop as twin-car 674/684 leaves and 685/675 approaches on 30 October 2008.

Opposite (bottom) Centenary car 645 unloads from both doors on 15 September 2011. This attractive colour scheme started life in March 2009 as an advertising livery for Jet2.com. Twelve months later the vinyls were removed and inverted V's added, inspired by the Sunderland livery applied to Balloon 703 (*see page 155*).

Supertram Stops

Above By 9 September 2011 the new Supertram platforms and shelter were ready, though unused. They were even further north, more Sandcastle than Pleasure Beach. Centenary car 647 - in its last two months of service - loads at the old stop, with a fragment of the 2008 Trueform shelter remaining.

Below Name-boards (in Times Roman lettering) were an interesting echo of Fleetwood Tramroad days. Centenary 642 waits in the rain on 10 October 2011.

Supertram Stops

The Supertram platforms opened for business on 4 April 2012.

Top Five weeks after the tramway re-opened, Flexity 011 draws up at the new shelter on 10 May 2012.

Centre The southbound platform still suffers from the limited pavement width that has plagued the Promenade ever since the reservation opened in 1903-5. The crews of Standard car 147 and Routemaster RML 2391 - old colleagues from the trams - exchange pleasantries on 18 August 2012.

Below A heavy downpour on 4 August 2012 has defeated the drainage. Flexity 014 decants passengers well-prepared for a showery afternoon on the Pleasure Beach. On the right is preserved Lytham PD/1 No. 19.

- 91 -

Heritage Stop(s)

Above When the Supertram system opened in April 2012, Blackpool Transport began running tours by heritage trams - in effect a revival of the old Promenade Circular. They ran between Pleasure Beach, where a retro-style stop was inaugurated on the inner circle, and Little Bispham. Balloon 706 loads on 27 May 2012.

Below As the heritage stop was in a rather inconspicuous position, a second stop was added in mid-May near the inspector's cabin - virtually a reincarnation of the old main-line stop which existed from 1937 to 1992. This one lasted only until the beginning of July, perhaps because - as happened elsewhere on the system - passengers mistook it for an ordinary stop. Balloon 717, seen on 1 July 2012, was restored in 2008 with the aid of a £100,000 legacy from Phillip R. Thorpe, whose name it bears.

Heritage Stop(s)

Above On 25 August 2013, Boat 600 shares the turning circle with No. 602, newly recommissioned and now carrying its original number (227) and a mythical – but much admired – Southport-style livery. Balloon 706 brings up the rear. (*Alan Robson*)

Below The heritage stop was used on the evening of 14 September 2012 for the launch of twin-car 272/T2 after restoration.

The Western Train

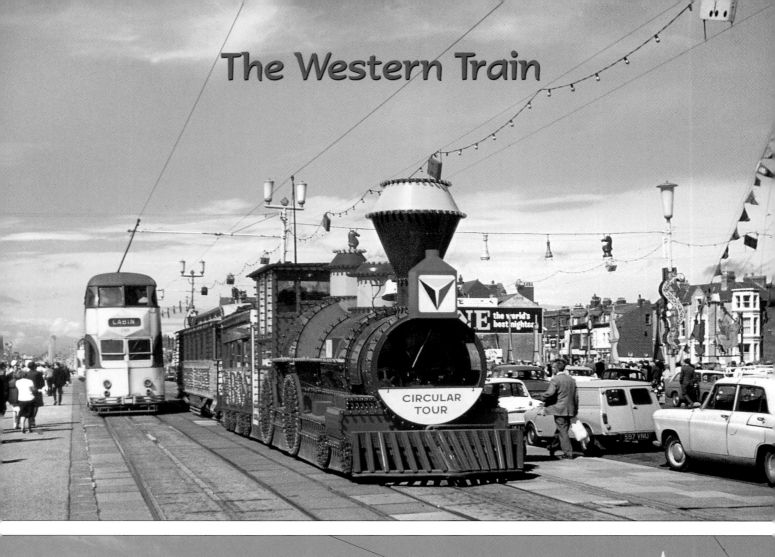

The heritage stop is also the starting-point for the Tour of Illuminations, often featuring one of Blackpool's iconic attractions - the illuminated Western Train.

Opposite (top) The Western Train approaches Pleasure Beach, while working a daytime Promenade Circular in August 1965. The Train was created in 1962 from railcoach 209 and Pantograph car 174, using a spare set of twin-car couplers.

Opposite (bottom) 47 years later the Train draws up at the heritage stop on 8 July 2012. Withdrawn in 1999, the Train was restored with Lottery funding and returned to service in 2009. The locomotive now runs on the frame of twin-car 677.

Above Room for a couple more, on 1 September 2012.

Right Waiting for the off. The clerestory roof was - appropriately enough - descended from the classic American railroad car, although it was distinctly old-fashioned by 1928, when the English Electric Company built the Pantograph cars to replace the old Fleetwood Tramroad saloons.

5. South Pier

South Pier was the terminus of the Promenade tramway from 1885 until 1903, when a 250-yard extension was opened to Pleasure Beach. It was known at first as *South Shore*, but became *Victoria Pier* when that structure opened in 1893, and *South Pier & Bath* when the pier was renamed in 1930.

South Pier became a junction when the Station Road tramway opened in 1897, though the connection was broken between 1903 and 1911, when it was restored for the phenomenally successful Circular Tour, which ran that way until 1932. After the Station Road tramway closed - along with the Squires Gate route - in 1961, South Pier ceased to have any operational significance.

Above Balloon 704 arrives at South Pier, followed by 720, on 29 June 1979. The southbound stop is the usual insignificant affair on the cramped footpath.

Railcoaches All

Top Railcoach 208 stands at the Station Road terminus of the Marton route in 1960. 208 was the test-bed for the Vambac control equipment and resilient-wheel bogies fitted to the Coronation cars, one of which is passing southbound on the Promenade.

Centre On 29 October 1961 – the final day of the tramway in Station Road – twin-car (ex-railcoach) 272 leaves South Pier for Central Station, travelling without trailer, as was the practice that winter. The north-to-east connection into Station Road is still intact, though there's no record of it being used, even by the most inveterate organiser of enthusiasts' tours.

Below Heading for South Pier after leaving Pleasure Beach, OMO car 8 (once railcoach 265) passes J.C. Robinson's imposing open-air baths on 24 February 1979.

Top OMO car 2 - in its last season - loads at the northbound stop on 6 July 1984, with a new pier entrance under construction.

Centre A few minutes later, Centenary car 641 heads south to Starr Gate on its first morning in service. Pablo's cafeteria is one of the oldest buildings in South Shore, starting life in 1849 as the Holy Trinity vicarage. James Pablo arrived from Bolton in 1906 as a street-sweeper, but soon became a leading light in the Blackpool ice-cream trade.

Below Balloon 701 stands at the northbound stop in June 1993. Its red and white livery was copied from Blackpool's pre-1933 colour scheme, which had been applied to six ex-London Routemasters (521-6). Two of these are passing - No. 522 (RM 848, new in 1961), with 525 (RM 1650 of 1963) in the background. After being withdrawn by Blackpool in 1996, both buses were sold to Reading Mainline, and then remarkably returned to London for further service. RM 1650 was still running there in 2014.

Above The northbound stop sign was curiously placed several yards back from the tracks. OMO 1 is going to be there quite a while on 10 August 1986.

Below After 111 years of exposure to the elements, northbound passengers at South Pier finally got some protection in June 1996, when an Abacus shelter was erected. To avoid obstructing the pier entrance, the stop was moved several yards south. Brush car 631, aptly advertising the *Laughing Donkey* family bar, passes on 25 October 2005.

New Stop and Shelter

In May 2009 the northbound stop was moved again, this time further north - indeed so far north that it was virtually where the Dean Street stop used to be many years ago. A Trueform Elite shelter - similar to that at Pleasure Beach - replaced the 1996 Abacus.

Top Twin-car 673/683 pulls up at the stop on 5 September 2010.

Centre Balloon 726 loads on 11 September 2010.

Below Brush car 632 leaves the new shelter to race Line 1 Trident No. 338 as far as the Cabin on 5 September 2010.

Above Passengers enjoy the sunshine on top of Marton Box car 31 as it passes Standard 147 loading at the north-bound shelter on 16 October 2010. The open-topper was on loan from Beamish Museum, where it has run since leaving Blackpool in 1984. Time was running out for the Trueform shelter, which disappeared the following month to allow the Supertram platform to be built on the site.

Below For the 2011 season, the stop – but not the shelter – moved back to the south of the pier entrance, where it had been from 1996 to 2008. On 18 July, Balloon 715 draws up at the stop. This new style of sign appeared at several stops from April 2011, but only lasted till November.

Supertram Stops

Above Flexity 010 loads at the northbound stop on 28 August 2012.

Centre Flexity 014 at South Pier on 4 August 2012. The distinctive building on the corner of Dean Street - described as 'in the Queen Anne style' - was contemporary with the tramway, being built in 1885 as three properties, capable of being converted into one.

Bottom Flexity 002 leaves the northbound stop on 8 June 2013. No. 002 was the least-used of the new cars, having spent six months of 2012 back in Germany. On its return to Blackpool, 002 was named *Alderman E.E. Wynne* after the Transport Chairman who was the driving force behind the closure of the street routes in the early 1960s. Make of that what you will.

6. South Promenade

There were four stops on South Promenade between South Pier and Manchester Square - at Waterloo Road, Alexandra Road, St Chad's Road and Barton Avenue. All but Barton Avenue received cast-iron shelters in 1925, and all had Adshels from 1972, and Abacus shelters from 1996. Only Waterloo Road and St Chad's Road survived 2011's cull of tram stops.

Above Standard car 147 approaches St Chad's Road during the procession to mark the 125th Anniversary of the tramway on 29 September 2010.

South Pier to Waterloo Road

Above On 19 December 1981, Brush car 634 and Balloon 701 (coupled together) ran up and down between Pleasure Beach and North Pier to keep the track grooves from freezing during the worst snow since 1947. The tram service was only running between North Pier and Ash Street, Fleetwood.

Centre Just leaving South Pier, Dreadnought 59 passes Brush car 621 alongside a crowded Promenade on 2 June 1985. Dean Street crossover stands out behind 621.

Bottom Much the same view – though slightly further north – 23 years later, with work under way to widen the Promenade. Balloon 709 passes Dean Street on 31 May 2008. 709 was rebuilt with twin-car style ends in 2000, and further rebuilt with new entrances in 2011.

Dean Street

Immediately north of Station Road was Dean Street, which until April 1942 had its own stop, and from 1911 to 1987 a crossover.

Above The crossover was in use from 20 January to 16 March 1979 during relaying between South Pier and Pleasure Beach. OMO car 9 prepares to reverse on 24 February.

Centre OMO No. 2 - at the limit of its fixed-head trolley - switches tracks on 24 February, with the help of an inspector stationed in a rather care-worn permanent-way hut. A few days later a temporary crossover wire was rigged up.

Bottom When the crossover was pressed into service again after an incident on 10 August 1985, trams with pantographs had be pushed across by trolley-fitted cars. Soon afterwards a permanent overhead wire was installed. OMO 8 is crossing on 20 April 1986, watched by an inspector with a smart Blackpool Transport van, but nothing much to do except to look after the single-line token.

Waterloo Road

Above On 6 July 1987 Balloon 723 is loading at Waterloo Road's Adshel, with 722 for Starr Gate approaching the 1982-style southbound stop. The 30 ft. high windmill was originally erected on top of the public toilets at Manchester Square for the 1928 Illuminations; it was moved to Waterloo Road in the 1950s and demolished in 2005. 723 had just lost an advertising livery, but only received part of its fleet colours. It ran in cream for the rest of the summer before being completed with green roof and bands.

Centre A close-up of the Adshel in August 1981, with Jubilee 761 loading.

Bottom The 1996 Abacus earning its keep on a rainy 16 May 2005, with rebuilt Balloon 724 approaching from South Pier.

Waterloo Road Crossing

Work began in July 2005 to widen the Promenade between South Pier and North Pier. Waterloo Road became an access point for vehicles serving the project, and a road crossing with traffic lights was installed just north of the tram stop.

Above Centenary car 643 passes through the traffic lights on 11 August 2007. The red and white barriers are to protect the overhead wire from high vehicles and vice versa.

Below There's nothing quite like a ride on an open-top tram. 602's passengers enjoy the experience as they leave the southbound stop on 31 May 2008.

Trueform Shelter

At the end of 2008, the Promenade works moved north of Waterloo Road, and the northbound stop could once again be provided with a shelter - a Trueform Elite, similar to that at South Pier.

Left On 11 April 2009, Standard car 147's guard supervises loading at the new shelter. Although the Balloons and Flexities operate with two guards, 147 has to manage - in traditional manner - with just one.

Below Half-term customers gaze in bemusement as Stockport 5 - pressed into use by a shortage of trams - pulls up at the Trueform shelter at dusk on 29 October 2009. The route-boards along the side of No 5 only compound the confusion of its destination display. On the left, Fleetwood Box 40 is also helping out.

Wide open spaces

Although the construction gangs had moved on, the landscapers had not yet arrived, and during 2010/11 a sea of temporary tarmac left Waterloo Road stop looking somewhat forlorn.

Above Liverpool 762 - on driver-training with a characteristic but cryptic destination - leaves behind another group of confused travellers at the Trueform shelter on 14 September 2010.

Below Balloon 715, newly repainted in 1970s livery but awaiting the correct style of fleet numbers, departs from Waterloo Road on 19 June 2011, passing the Supertram platforms slowly taking shape.

Flexities at Waterloo Road

At long last, the two great parallel projects – Promenade and Supertram – were finished, and on 4 April 2012 the Flexity cars began carrying passengers.

Top After a tramless winter, the local donkeys had established a right of way along the new track, and were in no hurry to relinquish it. Flexity 007 is about to pass one of the few west-side poles as it approaches Waterloo Road from South Pier on the first morning of Supertram operation.

Centre The completed Waterloo Road stop and landscaped Promenade seen from the north, with car 009 unusually heading for *The cabin* on 14 August 2012. Such non-standard destinations are entered on the driver's keyboard. During the driver-training period, a variety of exotic displays could be seen; one of the two training cars was seen showing *Blackpool F.C.*, while the other had *Preston North End*.

Below Flexity 013 on 28 August 2012 at the southbound platform, which – like most others – subsumes the entire footpath.

The Changing Scene

Almost half a century separates these views of southbound trams approaching Waterloo Road.

Top Second-series Balloon 253 (later 716) is followed by first-series 243 on 22 July 1964. Just visible on the left is Alexandra Road's 1925 cast-iron shelter. (*Peter Fitton*)

Centre Slightly further south, the open section of Manchester's 'California' car 765 is a fine spot for a Californian-style evening on 30 July 1985.

Below In the same place as 765 – at the start of the gentle curve – Standard car 147 on heritage duty approaches Waterloo Road, where Flexity 015 is just leaving on 2 August 2012.

Boats at Alexandra Road

There was quite a long gap – by Promenade standards – of about 400 yards from Waterloo Road to the next tram stop, at Alexandra Road. This is explained by the intermediate stop at Shaw Road having been closed in 1942 as a wartime economy measure.

Above Boat car 600 at the northbound stop alongside the Promenade works on 29 April 2007.

Below Southbound 606 passes Alexandra Road's Adshel in July 1981.

Alexandra Road

Above The latest OMO car, No. 12 - just converted from plastic-panelled railcoach 264/611 - approaches the southbound stop in the summer of 1975, with Balloon 716 following. (*Jean-Henri Manara*)

Centre Centenary 641 trails 645 and Balloon 706 past Alexandra Road in July 1988. 641's rear door is open - a common problem until the Centenaries were modified at their mid-life refurbishment.

Bottom Balloon 702 passes the Abacus shelter, which replaced the 1972 Adshel, on 17 May 2005.

At the end of the 2006 season the Abacus shelter was removed for the Promenade reconstruction works. Northbound passengers had to manage without a shelter until the stop was discontinued in 2008. The southbound stop survived until the end of July 2009.

St Chad's Road

Above Illuminated Standard car 159 has just left St Chad's Road on 22 July 1964, with Coronation 304 pulling up there. (*Peter Fitton*)

Centre The 1925 cast-iron shelter at St Chad's was replaced by an Adshel in 1972. OMO 10 (in an advertising livery uncannily similar to the crimson and yellow these cars first wore in 1972) loads on Centenary day, 29 September 1985. (*Peter Fitton*)

Below Minor repairs just south of St Chad's Road stop on 8 October 2004. Twin-car 673/683 on the Starr Gate - Fleetwood service, with Balloon 710 approaching from the north, and PW Bus 262 (*see page 122*) in attendance.

Above Twin-car 681/671 passes the St Chad's Abacus tram shelter, hemmed in by fencing as the new Promenade takes shape on 24 September 2006.

Below The track between South Pier and Manchester Square was completely rebuilt during the winter of 2006/07. Fleetwood Rack No. 2 approaches St Chad's along the new track during the 125th anniversary procession on 29 September 2010.

Beach Volleyball at St Chad's

The new Promenade curved out to sea opposite St Chad's Road to form what was called St Chad's Headland. Before it was landscaped, this was the venue for an International Beach Volleyball contest in 2008 and 2009. In addition to the well-known attractions of this sport, the top seats in the free stand afforded an excellent seagull's-eye view of the tramway.

Above Balloon 724 passes the entrance to the stadium on 10 September 2008.

Below Centenary 644 on 10 September 2009. The stop took its name from St Chad's Terrace (1891) in the background. Until 1892 St Chad's Road was Springfield Road.

Stops and Shelters

Right For the 2009 season, St Chad's was given one of the new Trueform shelters, as at Pleasure Beach, South Pier and Waterloo Road. Centenary 646 passes on 16 August 2010.

Below Like the other three locations, St Chad's only kept the shelter for two seasons before the Supertram platforms were built. The new stops were in the same place as the old, so for the 2011 season the stop - but not the shelter - was temporarily moved about 150 yards south to the other end of St Chad's Headland. Calling at this rustic-looking stop on Boat 600 was somehow reminiscent of happy days riding Llandudno toastracks through Bodafon fields. The date is 3 July 2011, and the Supertram platforms can be seen in the distance, with Balloon 711 approaching.

Stops and Shelters

Above By the end of the 2011 season, the landscaping had been finished, the barriers removed, and the stop looked a little more presentable, but not much. Centenary 647 loads there on 22 October, just two weeks before the old tramway finished, and the Centenary class with it.

Centre A close-up of the stop - still looking like a bunker on the Royal Lytham golf links - with 647 again, though this was two weeks earlier, on 7 October.

Bottom By contrast the Supertram platform was set in immaculate landscaped grounds. Balloon 715 passes, again on 7 October 2011.

Opposite (top) An unusually stylish hen-party waits for a northbound tram on 11 August, whilst Flexity 010 heads for Starr Gate.

Opposite (bottom) On 1 July 2012, Flexity 006 approaches the southbound platform.

St Chad's, 2012

St Chad's Road

Above The *B Fleet* comprises nine Balloons, rebuilt with projecting entrances to fit the Supertram platforms. They saw relatively little use in 2012, but 719 is calling at St Chad's on 2 November during half-term week.

Below Watching the Boats go by on 12 August 2012. The George Formby Society had recently paid for No. 604 to be repainted, renumbered and named. Discerning readers may detect the influence of the great French photographer Cartier-Bresson here. Or perhaps not.

The last stop before reaching Manchester Square was Barton Avenue. Unlike the others, it never had a cast-iron shelter, but did receive an Adshel in 1972, and an Abacus in 1996. The northbound stop and shelter were removed in 2008 when Promenade reconstruction work reached this point. The southbound stop lasted until July 2009.

Above The rarely-photographed northern end of Barton Avenue's Abacus shelter on 27 August 2001. Balloon 715 is southbound, while 710 approaches the stop.

Centre Balloon 701 at Barton Avenue on 30 May 1970, with Brush car 635 behind. 635 was withdrawn in 1974 for preservation, and is now at Crich awaiting completion of restoration to original 1937 condition as No. 298. 701 is still at Blackpool. (*Geoffrey Tribe*)

Bottom Not everyone's idea of a tram livery, perhaps, but Centenary 647's shocking pink provides a splash of colour as it leaves Barton Avenue on 12 March 2006. (*Paul Turner*)

Barton Avenue

Above The south end of the Abacus shelter on 2 April 2004 with 703 newly repainted in the 1980s livery which it first received retro-style in 1998, never having actually carried the livery in the 1980s.

Centre On the old Promenade, two ladies of leisure enjoy the early spring sunshine at Barton Avenue on 28 March 2002. Permanent Way gang bus No. 262 was formerly Fylde Borough Atlantean No. 92 and before that Hull 307. Blackpool acquired it with the Fylde undertaking in 1994. It served the tramway as PW bus from 2000 to 2006.

Bottom The new Promenade is under construction as David Beckham lets Jubilee 761 go by at the southbound Barton Avenue stop on 10 September 2008. 761 carried this livery from 2008 until it was sold for preservation in November 2011.

7. Manchester Square

Manchester Square was the junction for the Squires Gate route from 1894 until it closed on 29 October 1961, leaving only the short stretch of Lytham Road to Rigby Road depot. In January 1964, the crossover at Wellington Road was moved a couple of hundred yards north to permit cars to reverse at Manchester Square.

Above In the Spring of 1967, Brush car 289, working a Fleetwood - Manchester Square turnback service, reverses on the crossover.

A Winter Saturday

Above Low winter sunlight gives an unusually clear view of the equipment beneath Coronation 319, as it changes crew at Manchester Square on Saturday 9 December 1961.

Below A few minutes after the previous photograph was taken, railcoach 209 appeared, unexpectedly bearing the destination *Football Ground*. Everyone had assumed that football specials - once a great Blackpool tradition - had disappeared with the Lytham Road trams six weeks earlier. 209 unloaded its passengers in Lytham Road and, after the 2-2 draw with West Bromwich Albion, picked them up in Hopton Road. In the background can be seen the newly-installed manual pull for the frog at the junction, the automatic points having been removed when Lytham Road closed. Four months later, 209 was withdrawn to become the locomotive of the Western Train.

A Classic Tram Stop

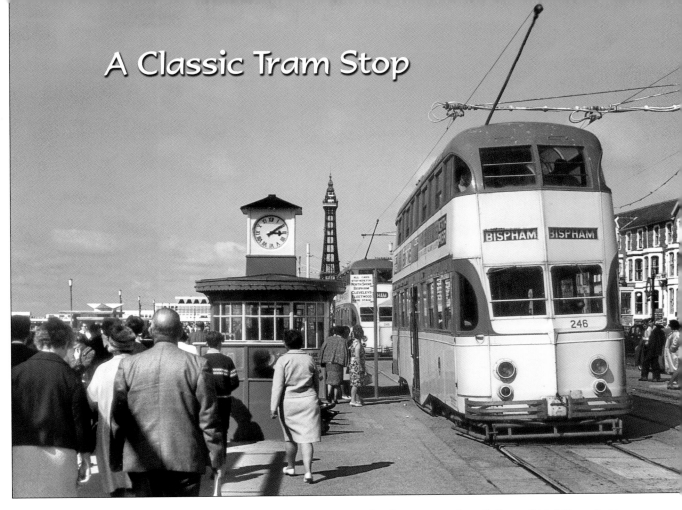

Above The tram stop at Manchester Square had barely changed for forty years when Balloon 246 followed sister car 248 to Bispham on 20 August 1967. The cast-iron shelter (by David Rowell & Co.) dated from 1911, and was originally on the east side of the track. The synchronised clock was added in 1926. (*Peter Makinson*)

Below Boat 606 leaves the southbound stop on 7 July 1968, with Balloon 720 behind and Coronation 652 at the shelter. Wind-screens (*left*) were first installed near tram shelters in 1924. They were made in the Corporation's own foundry, which went on to build complete cast-iron shelters from the mid-1920s. (*Peter Makinson*)

Above Standard cars 147 and 158 are heading for Promenade duty on 30 July 1966. The exodus of trams (plus coaches arriving at the Coliseum) produced this impressive jam alongside the Manchester Hotel.

Lytham Road

Below There was once a siding in the street outside the Manchester Hotel, which served as a terminus for the Lytham (and sometimes Marton) cars. Leaving the siding, they used a crossover by the hotel to reach the southbound line in Lytham Road. The siding was removed just before the Second World War, but the crossover remained to enable cars from Squires Gate to reach Rigby Road depot. After complaints of noise, it was removed in 1967. Coronation 321 passes the work site on 26 February.

Manchester Square Junction

Above Lytham St Annes No. 24 (a former Warrington Alexander-bodied PD/1 of 1946 vintage) gives way to Balloon 702 as it crosses onto the Promenade on 6 August 1970. (*David Christie*)

Below On 26 February 1967, Brush car 300 passes Karrier tower wagon 238, holding up a pole which is suffering under the weight of the junction wiring.

Enter the OMOs

The introduction of one-man service in October 1972 meant the end of the classic Blackpool tram stop and shelter at Manchester Square and elsewhere.

Top On 26 May 1973, the newest OMO car No. 6 - in service for just a month - is loading at the replacement Adshel, while experimental Brush OMO 638 approaches the southbound stop, with its new painted stop sign.

Centre At the beginning of 1973 a new junction (cast by Edgar Allen at a cost of £20,000) was put down. On 17 February OMO car 4 - formerly railcoach 220 - passes the usual perfunctory Health & Safety precautions. (*Geoffrey Tribe*)

Bottom The final OMO, No. 13 (ex-271/618) at Manchester Square on its first day in service, 17 June 1976. No. 13 carried this Brecknell Willis pantograph until April 1977, when it received a trolley.

- 128 -

All-over Advertising Cars

Above In 1975 OMO car 4 is followed by Balloon 707, which was Blackpool's first all-over advertising car. The sign-writer, having laboured long and hard to produce these 'balloons on a Balloon' was not best pleased when 707 became commonly known as the *Smartie Tram*.

Below The second advertising livery - for Blackpool Zoo, also in 1975 - appeared on Brush car 622 (*see page 71*) and the third on 634 to mark the centenary of the borough in 1976. 634 is seen here loading at the south-bound Manchester Square stop on its first day in service, 6 June.

The Manchester Hotel

Manchester Square took its name from a hotel which was built in 1846 as the Manchester House, and twice replaced.

Above For completeness, here is the original hotel, seen in 1922 with Lancaster car 14, and the cast-iron shelter still on the east side of the track. The hotel was demolished in 1935 and a new one opened the following year.

Centre On a damp Whit Monday afternoon, 28 May 1979, Balloons 719 and 715 pass outside the 1936 hotel, in a scene redolent of the long-departed Squires Gate route.

Bottom The 1936 hotel was demolished after sixty years. The third manifestation of the building provides a backdrop to Sheffield 513 and Fleetwood Box car 40 on 1 May 2005.

Snow Fighting

On 14 December 1981, Blackpool suffered its worst snowfall since 1947. Tram services were abandoned, while Balloon 722 and 723 (coupled together, with snowploughs at each end) tried to clear the track.

Above Having reached North Pier, the two cars returned to Rigby Road for reinforcements. 723 (with 722 behind) is crossing Manchester Square.

Below Setting out again, this time with 710 coupled between them. For more on this, see the author's *North Pier by Tram*.

Happy Anniversary

During the period covered by this book there were processions to mark the tramway's 75th, 100th and 125th anniversaries. The pictures on this page were taken as cars passed through Manchester Square to or from these various processions.

Top On 29 September 1960, Pantograph car 170 leaves Lytham Road to join the afternoon procession. 170 had taken lunch at Rigby Road after running from Bispham Depot to Pleasure Beach for the morning procession (*see page 70*).

Centre Conduit car 4, which led the 1960 and 1985 processions, waits at the traffic lights on 29 September 1985.

Below OMO car 8, which took part in 1985 and then rather gate-crashed the 125th Anniversary procession, returns to Rigby Road on 29 September 2010.

Adshel in Winter

The 1911 Rowell cast-iron shelter was replaced in 1972 by a standard Adshel as part of the OMO implementation.

Above A typical deserted winter scene in 1982. One-man car No. 3, the pleasure boat and the Adshel are all now just memories. The tram was scrapped in 1987, Blackpool's boats disappeared when insurance premiums soared after the *Marchioness* steamer disaster on the Thames in 1989, and the shelter went in 1996.

Below A lone passenger waits in the Adshel - more Ad than shel in this weather - for Centenary car 644 on 16 February 1994. The bench was a non-standard extra.

Back Home

Above On 15 October 2005, Balloon 700 heads for home, while 147 takes the easy route to Talbot Square, belying its evocative destination display.

Bottom The end of a day's work for the donkeys and Balloon 711 on 27 October 2009, as they wait to cross Manchester Square to their respective stables in Rigby Road.

Crossing Over

Top On 13 February 1981, OMO car 3 regains the southbound track after running wrong line from the Tower during relaying between Central Pier and Foxhall. Withdrawn PD/3 learner bus 378 serves as an inspector's cabin.

Centre From November 1986 the Promenade service was curtailed at Manchester Square whilst the crossover at Dean Street was superseded by a new one at the Pleasure Beach. Centenary car 641 has just reversed, while OMO car 7 is transferring its few passengers onto Atlantean 353 for the rest of their journey.

Below The traffic lights reveal the long exposure needed to capture OMO 11 with 641, which at the time (November 1986) was the only Centenary car in regular service.

Changing Crews

Manchester Square had been the change-over point for tram crews since 1935, when the new Transport Offices at Rigby Road opened.

Top Brush car 631's new driver settles into his cab, as an OMO driver waits with ticket machine and cash box at the northbound Adshel in September 1985.

Centre Restored Balloon 717 changes drivers on 18 October 2008.

Bottom Balloon 709's crew sort out a problem on 20 September 2010, while 719 approaches southbound.

Relaying the Junction

The junction at Manchester Square was relaid between January and April 2005, during which time cars went to and from the depot via Princess Street. The part-completed junction was briefly re-opened for Easter.

Top On a showery 24 March, twin-car 684/674 noses cautiously over the unpaved pointwork, watched by the proverbial one man and his dog.

Centre Only the southbound track into Lytham Road was ready for Easter. Rebuilt Balloon 724 crosses onto the Promenade on 28 March before reversing down to the crossover, and then reversing again to reach the northbound track.

Bottom The completed junction re-opened on the afternoon of 29 April. Standard car 147 is carrying out final tests.

The Abacus Shelter

The Manchester Square Abacus shelter, which replaced the Adshel in 1996, lasted until the end of the old system in November 2011.

Above On 8 September 2001, twin-car 673/683 pulls up at the northbound stop. Despite being made reversible in the 1960s, the twin-cars tended to stick to their original Pleasure Beach - Little Bispham itinerary.

Below Manchester Square's age-old propensity for flooding is demonstrated as Coronation 304 passes the Abacus on 23 September 2010.

Supertram Stops

The Supertram platforms were built north of the junction, nearly halfway to Foxhall Square, which lost its stop.

Right The platforms and shelter are nearly finished behind Brush car 632 and Balloon 715, which has stopped at the junction on 6 November 2011 - a green and cream farewell on the last day of traditional operation.

Below Centenary 648 passes the new stops on 26 October 2011. By the end of that year the sign had been replaced by the more traditional *Manchester Square*.

The New System

Top During 2012 and 2013 major work was carried out on the Manchester Square sewage pumping station. Balloon 709 approaches the site during a test run on 16 March 2012. No ordinary workmen these.

Centre 709 was one of the *B Fleet* - nine Balloons adapted with new entrances to fit the Supertram platforms, as seen here on 713 at Manchester Square on 21 July 2011.

Below The southbound Supertram platform was almost opposite Charles Crewe's Original Boarding Establishment of 1886 - Blackpool's first boarding-house (as opposed to company-houses where guests provided their own food). On 15 July 2012 Flexity 010 heads for Starr Gate - or in this case Starr Gate. The electronic display re-cycles about 100 times per second, so a faster shutter speed is likely to capture only a partial display.

- 140 -

Above Flexity 005 at the northbound Manchester Square stop on 2 August 2012. A destination of *Fisherman's Walk* (once more informatively shown as *Ash Street, Fleetwood*) was usually a sign of what French tramways call a *perturbation* in the service. There were quite a few perturbations in the summer of 2012, as the new system found its feet.

Below Driver's-eye view of Manchester Square on 6 April 2012, two days after the new service began, seen from Flexity 011, with just 604 kilometres on the clock.

'Twas ever thus

For all the money spent on the new sea defences, Manchester Square demonstrated on 3 January 2013 that when the wind blew and the tide was high, nothing much had changed.

Above These sandbags proved to be little more than a token gesture, and soon the entire tramway between Manchester Square and St Chad's was flooded. Flexities 013 and 001 pass four days later. (*Alan Robson*)

Centre Just before flooding stopped the tram service on 3 January, No. 008 splashes through water on the south side of the junction. (*Alan Robson*)

Bottom A century earlier, on 5 November 1911, one of the worst storms for twenty years scattered pleasure boats across the junction, holding up Marton Box cars 30 and 34 on their way from Blundell Street depot to take up service on the Marton route.

Trams and Buses

Manchester Square - like Pleasure Beach - became just a shadow of its former self once the Supertram system started. There were no longer any changes of crews or cars, and the only trams using the junction were occasional heritage cars going in and out of service.

Above Open-top Balloon 706 and a Stagecoach Trident on the 68 route to Preston wait their turns at the traffic lights on 2 August 2012.

Below On 15 July 2012, Fleetwood Box 40 forms a tableau of Promenade transport, with a landau and Routemaster RML 2391.

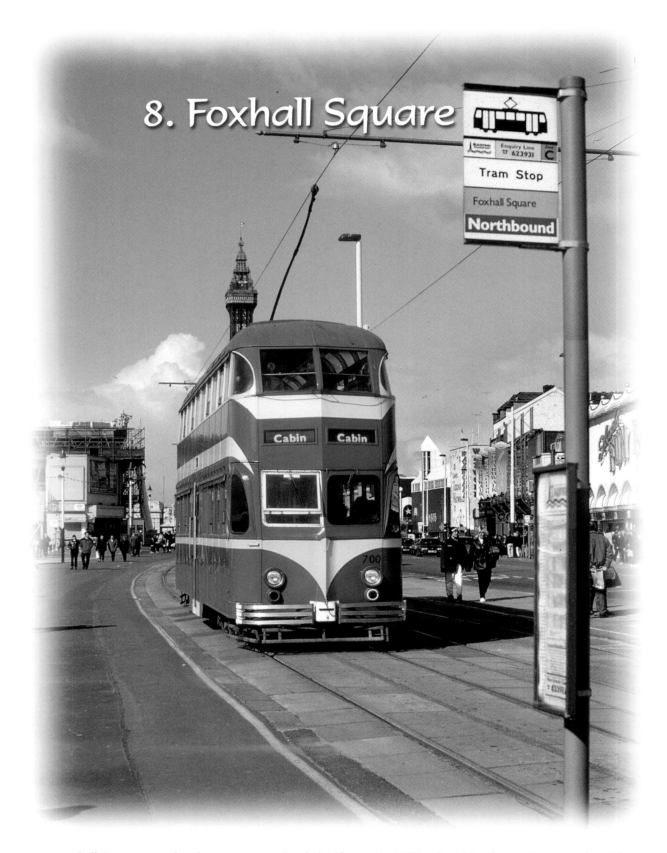

8. Foxhall Square

Foxhall Square ceased to have any operational significance in 1935, when Manchester Square replaced it as the access route to the depot and change-over point for crews, following the opening of Rigby Road depot. Nevertheless it still had great historical interest as the junction for the original depot line in Princess Street.

Above Balloon 700 leaves the 1990-style tram stop sign on 12 April 1998. 700 had been restored to wartime livery in 1997.

Foxhall
1960s

Above In July 1961 a slightly battered 147 rounds the curve from Central Pier as it nears Foxhall Square.

Centre Looking the other way at more or less the same spot, Coronation 319 heads north from Foxhall Square's cast-iron shelter on 26 October 1963. (*Geoffrey Tribe*)

Bottom Z-car Coronation 310 leaves Foxhall Square stop in the other direction on 28 December 1967. The Z-cars had their sophisticated Vambac equipment replaced by old Z4 controllers from scrapped railcoaches. On the right is the Foxhall Hotel, which dated back to the 18th Century - possibly earlier - but was shamefully demolished in 1990. (*Peter Makinson*)

Return of the Dreadnought

Top Dreadnought No. 59, which Blackpool had donated to the Crich Tramway Museum in 1965, returned in July 1975 to be restored by Blackpool Civic Trust, who displayed the car on the Promenade near the Foxhall that summer to raise funds for its restoration. (*Geoffrey Tribe*)

Centre After restoration, the Dreadnought was brought out for filming on 3 June 1976. As ever, this was a protracted business, and since the Dreadnought was holding up service cars, the enterprising decision was made to shunt it into Foxhall Square, which had not seen a tram for years. Here No. 59 is taking the points, which had probably not been used since 1964.

Below Coming back, the Dreadnought sets off from Foxhall Square. In the years that followed, No. 59 made several trips through Foxhall Square and along Princess Street on private tours.

1981
Contrasts

Above Just north of the Foxhall junction, coupled snowplough Balloons 723 and 722 make their way back to Rigby Road for reinforcements during the great snow of 14 December 1981.

Below At the same spot, on a hot July weekend, Balloon 709 passes the Adshel which replaced the 1925 cast-iron shelter in 1972. The crossover just north of the shelter had been removed in 1974.

One-man Operation

Top In January 1981 the track between Central Pier and Foxhall was relaid. OMO 11 passes, running wrong-line between Tower and Manchester Square.

Centre Centenary car No. 641, at the southbound stop on 22 September 1985. Oddly the north-bound Adshel has a smart painted 1972-style stop sign, while the southbound stop has a rather care-worn 1982-style sign with Brush car motif. (*Peter Fitton*)

Below Centenary 642 – just a month old – on 19 March 1987, passing the junction into Princess Street, which is being fitted with new points. PW Bus 258 (ex-337) is in attendance. (*Peter Fitton*)

- 148 -

Twin-cars at Foxhall

Above On 28 June 1998, for the centenary of the Fleetwood Tramroad, a special service ran from North Pier to Rigby Road via Princess Street, at a fare of £5, which often included a derailment en route. Twin-car 675/685 has come off at the Foxhall Square points. (*Peter Fitton*)

Below The Adshel was damaged in a gale on 26 January 1994, and subsequently demolished, leaving Foxhall shelterless for the rest of its life as a tram stop. Both stops were moved northwards in 1997. Twin-car 681/671 loads at the relocated stop on 21 August 2004.

Crossing the Prom

One of the highlights of the half-century covered by this book was the three-month period early in 2005 when trams went to and from Rigby Road depot via the historic track in Princess Street and Foxhall Square, while Manchester Square junction was relaid. Princess Street will have to wait for a later volume, but these two pages show some of the cars which traversed Foxhall Square.

Top Balloon 711 (on driver-training) prepares to cross the carriageway on 1 March 2005.

Centre The Kit-kat tram – Centenary 641 in one of its more popular advertising liveries – edges across the road, followed by works car 754 returning from its regular Saturday morning inspection of the line on 28 April.

Below The inspector has operated the special traffic lights for twin-car 682/672 to cross on a stormy 19 January.

In Foxhall Square

Above An unexpected participant in the fun and games was open-top Balloon 706, carrying a party of trainee guards on 28 April 2005. For reasons concerned with the overhead wire, cars with trolleys were shepherded through the streets.

Centre Cars with pantographs were left to find their own way back and forth, as with Brush car 626, moving out of Foxhall Square for a driver-training run on 22 April. When this new Foxhall replaced the old hotel, the official party for the opening on 29 July 1991 was carried by Boat car 606 from North Pier via Blundell Street and Princess Street to Foxhall Square.

Bottom Coronation 304 reverses in the square on 23 February, having made a test run from Rigby Road along Blundell Street and Princess Street.

New Track 2008

Top The track between Manchester Square and Central Pier was relaid during the winter of 2007/8. The new track made provision for the Supertram depot being in Blundell Street, and included two new crossovers. Brush car 630 makes the first trial run over the new north crossover at Foxhall on 19 March 2008.

Centre The second crossover, just south of the Foxhall, was of the facing variety to give access to a new point leading from the south into Princess Street. No overhead wire was installed, and no tram ever crossed over there, though 644 did its best on 14 May 2011 when the points on the southbound line were somehow left open. (*Gary Mitchell*)

Below Balloon 718 passes the new junction with the Princess Street line on 14 August 2008.

Birthday Guests

Above Oporto 273 in a Hitchcock-like setting at the Foxhall on 24 August 2010 during the Portuguese car's brief appearance for the tramway's 125th Anniversary.

Below Fleetwood Rack No. 2 meets Liverpool 762 near the turnout into Princess Street on 14 September 2010.

Above The open balcony of Standard car 40 approaching Foxhall behind a Boat car provides a grandstand view of the Promenade and tramway in August 1961. No. 304 is passing the cast-iron shelter, with another Coronation behind.

Below The same scene on 6 May 2008 with Centenary 645.

Foxhall Square

Top Approaching Foxhall from the south on 7 June 2010, Balloon 703 (in Sunderland livery) is running a farewell trip – without passengers – before leaving for Beamish museum.

Centre The northern crossover at Foxhall is often used to reverse the illuminated cars before they run down to Pleasure Beach to start their tours. The Western Train was on a daytime run to pick up a school party at Pleasure Beach on 27 June 2011.

Below If only. The new points for a southern junction into Princess Street were made redundant by siting the depot at Starr Gate. On 8 June 2012 Balloon 718 approaches on its first test run since being widened.

The new northern junction was never used either, and the wires into Foxhall Square were disconnected in April 2013 and removed altogether in October.

Looking for all the world like a southbound tram shelter, this is in fact the northbound shelter for the No. 5 bus. The shelter is long gone, as is bus 382; the No. 5 bus still runs, but not past Central Pier. Coronation 327 survives, awaiting restoration. On the left is the new pier entrance, replacing one from 1928. It still exists, though the lifeboat-house beyond it went in 2009.

Central Pier Tram Stops

Jubilee 761 loads at Central Pier's northbound stop on 2 June 1980. 761 had entered service in July of the previous year after being re-constructed from Balloon 725.

Above A well-dressed queue waits to board 707 at the new Brush-car stop sign on a warm August evening in 1982. The Balloon is already wearing its third advertising livery since 1975, and didn't regain the dignity of green and cream until 1998.

Below Pulling up at the southbound Brush-car sign in August 1982 is - appropriately - the first of the Brush cars, No. 621 (ex-284).

Swap Shop

Above In November 1998 Boat car 606 was painted in the blue and yellow of the associated Seagull Coaches fleet. It is approaching the relocated northbound stop at Central Pier on 7 May 2000 during a run to Cleveleys – an unusually long trip for a Boat.

Centre In September 2000, No. 606 made a much longer trip to Cleveland, Ohio, in exchange for Standard car 147, whose halogen headlamp is piercing the gloom of a dismal 5 November 2005 as it passes the pier entrance.

Bottom 147 then pulled up at the northbound Abacus shelter which had finally - after 113 years - been installed in October 1998. Even then it was second-hand, having been displaced by reconstruction work on New South Promenade. For a few days it still carried the name *Harrowside*, and, for the rest of its life, until removed in 2010, never bore the name *Central Pier*.

Above In 2011, to allow the Supertram platforms to be built, the two stops were moved back to their old positions outside the pier. That season's much-curtailed service (between Pleasure Beach and Little Bispham only) is causing some confusion to passengers boarding - or not - trailer 685 at the northbound stop on 10 July.

Below A bit cold for boating, but 600's passengers and crew are well wrapped up as they pass the new Supertram platforms on 26 October 2011, eleven days before the old system closed.

Top The old southbound Central Pier stop had only another week to serve when Marton Box car 31 loaded there on 27 October 2010.

Centre : The new southbound stop – for 2011 only – was on the site of the pre-1968 stop (*see page 156*) opposite the pier entrance. Centenary 642 loads by the new stop sign (also for 2011 only).

Below The northbound stop was immediately opposite the southbound. On 26 October, Standard car 147 loads passengers for a short trip to North Pier. Apologies for featuring 147 again, but its rear entrance is very amenable to tram-stop pictures. And it *is* a very photogenic car.

Opposite (top) On 24 August 2013, Flexity 016 loads at Central Pier's northbound platform.

Opposite (bottom) Flexity 014 at Central Pier, bound for Bispham on 28 September 2013.

- 162 -

Supertrams by day ...

... and night

The half-mile of amusement arcades, stalls and sideshows on Central Promenade, between Central Pier and the Tower, is known - apparently without irony - as the Golden Mile. Although there is little intrinsic tramway interest, it remains an iconic stretch of track, where the trams can be seen in their essential Blackpool environment.

Above The Golden Mile and tramway on 26 July 1963.

Opposite In complete contrast, OMO car 13 has Central Promenade to itself on 26 January 1979.

The Changing Mile

Opposite (top) The Golden Mile as it had been since the 1920s, with Coronation 308 running the main Fleetwood service on 27 October 1963. (*Geoffrey Tribe*)

Opposite (bottom) The Mile partly modernised in 1968. Railcoach 616 was withdrawn two years later to become OMO car 1.

Top Boat 235 running the Promenade Circular - basically a daytime Tour of Illuminations - on 20 August 1967. (*Peter Makinson*)

Centre Balloon 709 heading north from Central Pier on 20 July 1968.

Below On 12 June 1976, the restored Dreadnought appeared in a procession to mark the Centenary of the Borough. Here it is running up to the Tower to reverse. Temporary sideshows occupy part of the old Golden Mile.

Golden Mile Scenes

Left Snowplough 723 trying to clear the southbound track on 14 December 1981.

Below Standard car 40 sets out along the Golden Mile on 1 October 1985, with Balloon 716 approaching the southbound stop.

Opposite (top) Balloon 721's unusual half-and-half advertisement for Michelin Tyres is completely overshadowed by the spectacular Thunderbirds rocket on 15 October 2004.

Opposite (bottom) Centenary car 646 stands at the Abacus shelter on 17 April 2006, while Fleetwood Box car 40 heads south.

Checkpoint Charlie

Top The illuminated Trawler was one of the first cars to run when the tramway reopened as far as North Pier on 20 April 2011 after a winter shut-down. Here the former Brush car (633) is waiting at Central Pier for permission to proceed.

Centre For the first few weeks of the 2011 season, trams between the lifeboat-house and North Pier ran behind barriers, manned by security guards. To add to the Berlin-like atmosphere, trams didn't stop – not even at the Tower. The best way to see what was going on was to take a ride through the blockaded area - in this case on Brush car 632, approaching the Tower northbound on 29 April 2011.

Below The security guard releases Balloon 717 into the community at the lifeboat-house barrier on 27 April 2011.

Opposite (top) The completed Central Promenade, with newly restored Centenary car 648 running a heritage trip on 24 August 2013.

Opposite (bottom) A morning sea mist gives a different look to a familiar scene on 24 May 2012.

11. The Tower

The journey from Starr Gate ends - for now - at the Tower, a location which the next volume in this series will cover in more detail. The following pages give just a flavour of the place.

Above The Tower stop on 22 June 1980, with Balloon 707 loading at the southbound shelter.

Opposite (top) Trams to the Tower were once so familiar that books were named after them. Now they're a rare sight, except when the service is cut back for an event on the Tower Headland, as with 003 on 31 August 2012.

Opposite (bottom) A Lowry-esque view of 012 at the northbound Tower platform on 30 July 2012. New tramway, new trams, new Promenade, new carriageway - same old sea and sands.

The Tower

Above Recruits being schooled in the gentle art of snatching a quick smoke at the terminus - in this case the Tower, with Balloon 706 on 14 May 2008.

Below H.R.H. Prince Edward inspects the new Comedy Carpet, having arrived via Flexity 001 - even newer - on 7 February 2012. (*Alan Robson*)